fP

MAGNETIC PARTNERS

Discover How the Hidden Conflict
That Once Attracted You to Each Other
Is Now Driving You Apart

STEPHEN J. BETCHEN

FREE PRESS

New York   London   Toronto   Sydney

FREE PRESS
A Division of Simon & Schuster, Inc.
1230 Avenue of the Americas
New York, NY 10020

First Free Press hardcover edition May 2010

FREE PRESS and colophon are trademarks of Simon & Schuster, Inc.

For information about special discounts for bulk purchases,
please contact Simon & Schuster Special Sales at 1-866-506-1949
or business@simonandschuster.com.

The Simon & Schuster Speakers Bureau can bring authors to your live event.
For more information or to book an event contact the Simon & Schuster Speakers Bureau
at 1-866-248-3049 or visit our website at www.simonspeakers.com.

DESIGNED BY ERICH HOBBING

Manufactured in the United States of America

10 9 8 7 6 5 4 3 2 1

Library of Congress Cataloging-in-Publication Data
Betchen, Stephen J.
Magnetic partners: discover how the hidden conflict that once attracted you
to each other is now driving you apart / Stephen J. Betchen.
p. cm.
1. Couples—Psychology.   2. Married people—Psychology.
3. Interpersonal conflict.   4. Marital conflict.   I. Title.
HQ801.B4953 2010
616.89'1562—dc22   2009041175

ISBN 978-1-4516-1403-9

NOTE TO READERS

Names and identifying details of individuals portrayed in this book have been changed. In most instances, persons portrayed are composites.

To my clients past and present—
You all share in the success this book may bring
in relieving the suffering of couples

CONTENTS

MAGNETIC PARTNERS

1

THE MAGNETIC POWER
OF MASTER CONFLICTS

If there's one thing I've learned about relationships in my thirty years of doing couples therapy, it's that they're *complex*. We'd all like to think that we fall in love, choose a life partner, and then the rest is as effortless as riding a bike. But the truth is that relationships require a constant job of adapting, compromising, and keeping pace with our partners so that we avoid growing apart—and that is the easiest piece of the puzzle. The hardest is usually beyond our level of consciousness: I'm talking about knowing ourselves. We must start out with personal insight and an understanding of how we were influenced by our pasts. What's driving us to do the things we do? What's compelling us to feel the way we feel? And, as I'll encourage you to explore as the special focus of this book, what inner conflicts are a constant struggle for you?

Some people may be in relationships that are all smooth sailing. Maybe the stars are aligned in their favor, and these couples have somehow managed to control their conflicts. It could also be true, however, that they've decided to settle, not wanting to rock the boat because they don't believe that a better deal awaits them.

And, of course, there are those who are afraid to change. After all, change is hard, and for most of us, relationships are tough to manage. But I don't say this with pessimism. I'm actually a confirmed optimist, and a big believer in relationships. I'm stressing the difficulty involved because in my practice I've seen too many couples give up too easily on their relationships. I'll never forget one newlywed who decided to divorce her husband after six months because she felt that a "normal marriage should be easy." Again, not true. To achieve relationship success, you've got to be patient, be committed, and work hard. In his book *Way of the Peaceful Warrior,* Dan Millman wrote: "Stress happens when the mind resists what is." In *Magnetic Partners,* we will face reality together.

Through the course of this book, I will share with you my strongest conviction as a couples therapist: an underlying, largely unconscious conflict is responsible for most of the truly intractable relationship problems I've helped couples through. Affairs, chronic fighting, troubled sex lives, and most dating dilemmas, I have found, very often can be traced to what I have come to call a "master conflict," a powerful conflict that largely controls your relationship. What's more, this same master conflict has very often also acted as a powerful bonding force in the relationship. The great irony about master conflicts is that they are often the underlying force of attraction that brought a couple together with an almost magnetic power, and yet, just as often, the same force is pushing a couple apart.

What is a master conflict? Think of it as an unconscious struggle within yourself—like having two politicians inside you, arguing about some issue, and you just can't make up your mind as to whom you should believe. The especially tricky thing about this struggle is that one politician is not necessarily right and the other wrong. In this struggle, neither side is necessarily better than the other. But even in those situations when one side does seem to be the more appropriate choice, those two politicians in your head are both scoring points, enough to confuse you—blurring the difference between right and wrong and making it even more difficult for you to make a decision. For example, you may be conflicted about being either powerful or passive in your relationship: *being in charge* is gratifying but too much work; *being passive* leaves you with little responsibility but too little control. Or you might be conflicted about meeting your needs: *taking care of yourself* may feel good but evoke guilt; *taking care of your partner* may be the right thing to do but may also lead to too much responsibility.

Trying to reach a compromise with your master conflict is usually no easy task. Why? Because compromise means change, and change usually brings with it the anxiety of taking on the unknown and the depression that comes with a loss of the way things were. But there is good news: these feeling-states are usually temporary, so if we can tolerate them, they may lead us to a much better life, one that we never could have imagined. What I'm saying is that underlying fear—the fear of anxiety and depression—makes it difficult for us to choose one side over the other or to strike some sort of compromise between the two sides. Shifting back and forth helps us to avoid the pain that might come from making a choice. Why take charge in your relationship if you fear having too much responsibility? Why be passive if you fear being controlled? Master conflicts can cause us pain, but to avoid discomfort we prefer not to challenge them; we prefer to "stay the same without the pain," and who can blame us? We may seek help to stop the suffering but not to change the internal master conflict. I'll show you what I mean.

Take the case of Seth, who at age fifty-five was still a bachelor, though in a painful, dead-end relationship. He couldn't move on because a master conflict had a tight grip on him; he was torn by the inability to decide whether to commit to a lasting relationship or to remain free of the responsibilities that such a relationship requires.

He slowly shuffled into my office one day and began to tell me his story in a soft, monotone voice. He was dating Denise, thirty-nine, a tall, lanky graphic artist whom he wanted to marry. But Denise gave Seth numerous signs that she wasn't genuinely interested in him—canceling dates at the last minute and acting preoccupied when they were together. Most of us have been subjected to indifference at least once in our dating careers; it's no fun at all. It's also not at all hard to pick up on. Seth's friends could clearly see the truth; they had told him that they felt Denise wasn't the least bit interested in him, pointing out that she saw him only when she had nothing else to do and that she refused to have sex with him. But Seth had brushed off their comments. Then one night his cousin Barb joined the happy couple for dinner, and afterward she told Seth: "There's no way that girl likes you. My God . . . she seemed more interested in watching the restaurant television than hanging out with you. Women know women . . . you dip! Forget about her." That hit Seth hard, and shortly after this he came to see me.

As I talked with Seth, I quickly discovered that he wasn't at all clueless about how Denise was treating him. The real problem was that her indifference actually suited one side of his master conflict just fine. He was under the sway of the *commitment vs. freedom* conflict, which led him to *commit* to distant and "unavailable" women and to *reject* other, more available, female partners, thereby

4

guaranteeing his freedom. It was his unconscious way of not having to choose between commitment and freedom.

When I pointed his conflict out to him, he resisted the notion. "Listen, I want to be married," he said to me, "I'd like nothing better. I'd love to marry Denise." But, like most people who are in the grip of a strong conflict, Seth blamed his partner. "Denise keeps her distance: I just can't pin her down," he said. Okay, but even when I advised him of his futile situation, he refused to move on. His excuse: "I'll never find another woman my age as hot as Denise." Our master conflicts are powerful motivators for rationalization. The point is that Seth chose to continue a painful charade with Denise rather than give her up and risk commitment with a more eligible partner.

Some people liken the struggle to make a choice—the key characteristic of master conflicts—to being on a seesaw with an issue at each end. When you lean toward choosing one side of the conflict, the seesaw is weighted toward that end; when you lean toward the other side of the conflict, the seesaw is weighted toward the other end. And you just keep tipping back and forth! Couples usually run into trouble when the seesaw is tipped too far toward one end. If it stays unbalanced for an extended period of time, then the sparks can really fly. For example, if a couple were able to deftly balance a conflict about closeness, they might be able to get by with only a few minor skirmishes. But if one partner decided to tip the seesaw by demanding a great deal more or a great deal less closeness, the relationship would probably end up in serious trouble. That is, unless the other partner shifted as well.

Do you remember this story? When Viagra, the drug for erection problems, first became available, a woman sued her seventy-year-old, longtime lover for damages. The woman claimed that the lover had been impotent for four years, but once he regained potency with the help of Viagra, he dumped her for another woman. I'm sure there's more to the story, but my point is that for most of their four years together I suspect the couple was able to balance a master conflict centered around a serious sexual issue. But the feisty boyfriend tipped the seesaw beyond return when he suddenly decided to become potent and ply his wares elsewhere.

I am sympathetic about the anxiety that accompanies the decision-making process about a deep conflict—I've had my own big ones to grapple with over the years. When a person is truly struggling with one of these conflicts, it can seem as if his or her very survival depends on striking a good compromise.

This is where the power of master conflicts to bring couples together comes into play. They often act as a powerful—and almost immediate—bonding force.

The conventional wisdom holds that opposites attract. Well, on a surface level, opposites *do* attract. But, on a deeper and more important level, opposites *do not* attract—an assertion that at first confuses most of the couples I counsel, who believe they're fighting so much because they're so different. Certainly, we are often drawn to people whose personalities or temperaments are different from ours in certain ways, and those differences can lead to conflict. If you're excitable or prone to stress, you may consciously pick a partner who you're convinced is the complete opposite—calm. You may then end up fighting because your partner's calmness begins to seem to you like a sign of not caring as much about things as you do, or because your partner begins to find your behavior agitating or hysterical. The psychological and biological (neurological and hormonal) makeup of men and women is different in some ways, though I believe that biological and gender differences have been overstated and that a stronger, deeper force of attraction in most of the couples I've counseled has been a shared master conflict. Again and again in my couples counseling, I've found that underlying conflicts play a major role in our choice of a long-term mate.

The reason master conflicts act as such a magnetic force is that in order to maintain your conflict, which almost all of us unconsciously try desperately to do, you *must* select someone with the same or similar conflict—your "twin-in-conflict." If you pick someone with an identical conflict—unconsciously, of course— you can avoid resolving the conflict, and your partner can act as a fail-safe in this effort. After all, it's natural that we feel most comfortable with someone who shares our master conflict because, on a deeper level, this person "gets" us and we also get them. Your unconscious quickly tells you that this person has experienced what you've experienced; therefore, what's most important to him or her is most important to you.

Okay, you might ask, but what about physical attraction? What about personality type? What about similar interests? Don't these factors count for anything? Of course they do. I strongly believe they all help us make relationship choices—just not in the same way that we often think they do. For example, if you're a woman who is attracted to tall men with dark hair, I'm sure you look for these characteristics when searching for a mate. This is "surface attraction"—and it will take a relationship only so far. For a deep bond to occur, you'll need to find a tall, dark man with whom you're also compatible, and one of the powerful sources of compatibility is a shared master conflict.

Your master conflict is, by far, the best matchmaker you've got. For better or for worse, dating sites don't come close to your master conflict. It even probably dictates whom you will choose on these popular sites. I tell clients this all the time: If I put you in a room with one hundred people, there's an excellent chance that you'll unconsciously choose the person with a similar master conflict. And let me stress that this is not necessarily a bad thing.

THE PROS AND CONS
OF THE MASTER CONFLICT

Master conflicts are normal in relationships and totally unavoidable. They exist in even the healthiest couples, but they rarely cause severe damage to these relationships. Some couples are simply better able to tolerate anxiety and loss and to successfully negotiate with their conflicts, and they experience only minor eruptions in their relationships.

Master conflicts also can do a couple some good. They can, at times, help to balance a relationship by limiting extreme behavior. For example, one partner might be able to set some limits on the other's excessive spending and keep the couple financially solvent; the spendthrift may inject some much-needed excitement and fun into an otherwise boring relationship. But in many couples, master conflicts eventually become toxic to the point of destruction.

Take the case of a couple I treated, Eric and Jenna, who shared a *security vs. risk* conflict.

Jenna walked briskly into my office and threw herself down on one of the soft blue chairs by the window. At thirty-six, she was an attractive real estate agent. She immediately came across as decisive and fast-paced, speaking in a frustrated, pressured tone. "Life is so boring with Eric. I can't stand it. I feel like I'm dying a slow death. He just doesn't show any passion for anything, especially our sex life. There's not an ounce of spontaneity in him—he's so controlled."

Eric was one of those souls who had a smile permanently attached to his face, as if someone had come along and *glued* a grin on him.

While still smiling, Eric protested his wife's remarks. "We do a lot of things together—you're just insatiable," he said. "Yes, it's true that I don't like to take big risks or just take off somewhere without having a plan, but I enjoy life. I also like sex; I'm just not as kinky as you. Actually, I think you're a little weird." Eric then turned to me and said, "Jenna can never be satisfied. She's an out-of-control Energizer Bunny." When I asked him to clarify, he responded: "Jenna lives by the seat of her pants. If it were up to her, we'd live like Romans, but we wouldn't have a penny left to our name."

Eric and Jenna seemed to be complete opposites, but underlying their differences was the powerful psychological bond of both being conflicted about the degree of life security they wanted to get from being with a partner versus the amount of risk they wanted to take in their lives. Jenna vaguely knew she was attracted to Eric's stable personality. But she had no idea that she'd soon become bored by stability and desperate for more stimulation. After all, no matter how stressful and disorganized her childhood had been, it never lacked excitement, risk, and unpredictability. In a sense, Jenna didn't realize it when she married, but her internalized conflict dictated that she needed it both ways: unlimited excitement in her life as well as a safe, stable environment—two opposing needs. When things were too stable, she grew bored and looked to shake things up by engaging in risky, stimulating behavior; for example, Eric once caught Jenna looking at a dating site on the internet. When things were too out of control, she became anxious and sought stability and security. Most of the time she shifted back and forth, trying to find some sort of balance or compromise between the two. But since that wasn't quite satisfying enough, she was threatening to end the marriage.

Eric knew that he was attracted to Jenna's exciting, spontaneous personality, but he didn't realize that it also scared him because it threatened to disturb his sense of order. He too was unaware that his internalized conflict dictated that he needed it both ways: excitement and spontaneity, but without risk—also two opposing needs. When Jenna randomly decided to spend a large amount of money on a luxurious car or pressured Eric to take a spontaneous trip to an exotic land, his anxiety level would blow sky-high. But if she failed to find something stimulating for the couple to do for some period of time, Eric became bored, somewhat immobilized, and slightly depressed. He too was trapped by his master conflict.

Eric and Jenna's relationship wasn't always this tense. For the first two years of marriage they were able to keep their *security vs. risk* master conflict under control by seesawing back and forth. For example, Eric would mildly pressure Jenna to curb her spending but willingly participated in many of her activities. He even took a vacation to Rio de Janiero with her that included only one minor skirmish, when Jenna wanted to extend the trip a few more days. Eric found this excessive but called their travel agent and booked the trip for an extra three days. Jenna also didn't rock the boat too hard in the beginning of the marriage. She was never at a loss to try new and exciting things, but aside from the trip, she was generally careful about her spending. At times she even expressed concern about the couple's finances, and this was music to Eric's ears. So what happened? If Eric and Jenna were able to hold their master conflict in check at the beginning of their marriage, how did the relationship deteriorate to the point that they badly needed professional help? How did their marriage nearly fall apart so fast?

Many couples ask me these questions. The truth is that most relationships deteriorate over time if master conflicts aren't under the control of the couple—they must be well managed. In the beginning, as in Eric and Jenna's case, there are usually subtle signs that bigger problems are on the horizon. Examples are minor disagreements about the same issues over and over, such as how to handle money or how often to have sex. But these disagreements gradually begin to grate on each partner and grow increasingly unmanageable. Add to this an increase in life stressors such as the buying of a house, having children, or establishing careers, and a couple can develop serious problems before they can say "marriage counselor." True, Eric and Jenna were able to balance their master conflict at the start of their relationship, but the balance proved to be a delicate one. Eric did enjoy Jenna's ability to have fun and throw caution to the wind, but he lived in fear of her. Every time she took a risk he worried not only about the immediate consequences but about the future as well. He wondered what expensive venture Jenna would come up with next. He eventually became so unnerved that he developed a flinch response whenever she approached him. He thought, Now what does she want? How much will it cost? And even though Jenna enjoyed Eric's practical nature, every time he questioned her moves, she resented him a little more. Soon she saw him as a "parent" trying to sap the enjoyment out of her life. With every passing year Eric worried more and more about whether the couple would have enough money saved for retirement, while Jenna worried about life passing her by.

So, do Eric and Jenna have any hope? Absolutely! Usually when partners realize that they actually share the same conflict, they begin to empathize with each other rather than fight. Anger, blame, and criticism subside greatly and I've found that husband and wife can become close allies, connected in a way that they've never experienced before. At that point, partners also tend to focus more on the positive aspects of each other's personality rather than the negative aspects. Tolerance levels increase and negotiation and compromise come much more easily. Eric, for example, learned to focus more and more on the value of Jenna's vivacious personality and the richness she brought to his life. Whereas he had begun to say no to Jenna before she even finished a sentence, he now learned to listen and carefully evaluate the merits of her suggestions. Jenna came to value Eric's desire for stability more than she ever had. She began to think longer-term, and when Eric attempted to veto one of her ideas she handled it with grace and maturity. In a sense, both partners took responsibility for the problems they had brought to their relationship rather than blame each other.

Eric and Jenna turned out just fine but, like all couples, they had other options. They could have let their relationship continue as it was, but in my experience in counseling, the frictions over their master conflict would have continued to escalate and most likely they'd have ended up divorced. They could also have decided to give in to their master conflict, cut their losses, and move on. Unfortunately, it is also my experience that couples who ignore their master conflict are only inviting it to wreak havoc in their next relationship.

In working with couples, I have found that the extent to which a master conflict will cause trouble in a relationship will depend on several factors:

- *The strength of the master conflict and the depth of the couple's pain.* *The influence of the master conflict almost always depends on the couple's perception of how difficult it is to endure and their threshold for pain. In some cases, one partner may be much less tolerant than the other, and this can lead to a quick separation or divorce.*

- *How long the master conflict has been causing the couple problems.* *If you have a large cavity and you don't get it filled, you may end up needing a root canal; if you don't get a root canal, you may end up losing the tooth. Likewise, if an unruly master conflict is allowed to simmer, pain and loss will follow.*

- *Each partner's ability to recognize the conflict and to take personal responsibility for his or her contribution to it, rather than assign blame to each other.* *The more perceptive the couple and the less defensive each partner is, the better their chance of managing their master conflict.*

- *Each partner's communication skills and problem-solving capability.* *We learn these skills in our families of origin. The better our parental role models were in these areas, the better our skills are.*

- *How badly a couple wants to stay together.* *Some partners have "one foot out the door," and they know it. Couples have to work hard at managing their master conflict; less than a full commitment will probably be a waste of time.*

- *How badly a couple wants to be healthy.* *Staying together is one thing; plenty of couples allow their dysfunctional master conflicts to live on indefinitely. By contrast, a strong desire to be healthy means that you not only want to maintain the relationship, you want to be fulfilled by it as well.*

- *How healthy a couple is capable of being.* *The simple truth is that some people just can't fix their problems. These couples need to weigh the damage an out-of-control master conflict is inflicting on them, and then seriously consider whether it's worth staying together.*

Make no mistake, our conflicts can cause us a great deal of pain, especially when we reach a juncture where they are producing actual conflict of the kind Jenna and Eric were having. Couples for whom this is happening must learn to manage their shared conflict more successfully. In order to begin better management, we must first come to a better understanding of the nature of master conflicts, and then diagnose the issues in our own relationship specifically, and that is what this book will help you to do. To start that process, first let's look more deeply into the nature of master conflicts, where they come from, and the basis of my argument about the role they play in relationships. Master conflicts are never completely resolved—they're too deeply ingrained in us. But you can have a great relationship if you first find out what your master conflict is and then get it under your control.

THE PSYCHOLOGICAL BASIS

I'll probably sound like Woody Allen when I say this, but my analyst once told me that "conflict makes the world go around." What did he mean by this? "We all have desires that we'd like to gratify," he explained, "but we can't always get what we want—or the price we'd have to pay to satisfy these desires seems just high enough to create conflict in us." Remember those two politicians inside of you, creating a mass of frustration and confusion? Well, it's a common, natural occurrence to be constantly confronted with situations that compel us to ask ourselves what is the right thing to do, or what's the best path to take, or whether it's worth the effort to go after what we want.

My point is that conflicts are a fundamental part of the human psyche, and so we all have them. How many people do you know who are completely satisfied with their life choices? Not many, I'll bet. I can't tell you how many guys I've met in their fifties who still want to be rock stars. *Intellectually* they've accepted the fact that they'll never play an instrument on a stadium stage, but *emotionally* their fantasies may live on, creating a real malaise for themselves about life. I did not perceive right away in my counseling of couples how looking into their conflicts as individuals could provide such a powerful explanation of the relationship crises I was seeing. The core insight about how inner conflicts might be at play came to me unexpectedly, when I was in a therapy session myself.

I decided to open my own private clinical practice in the fall of 1992, after many years of training in couples therapy. I ended up treating just about every type of couple and every relationship problem you could imagine. My practice was thriving, but over time I became bothered by the fact that some couples weren't progressing as well as I'd expected. I told myself that I had to go deeper; I had to do a better job of figuring out what was keeping these couples from resolving their problems. So, I went into psychoanalytic training to study the deepest form of psychotherapy treatment.

I was in session, lying on the couch, as one is required to do in analytic training, and I mentioned to my analyst that I was considering writing a book on a specific type of relationship dynamic that had caught my interest. In response, after a long pause, he simply said, "Hmmm." Six months later I brought up the book idea again. This time my analyst let out a throat-clearing grunt. After about a year's time had passed, I brought the subject up a third time. This time his response was priceless. He shot back at me, "You could have written it by now." That comment really made me think; I was forced to ask myself a simple but vital question: *If I wanted to do something, why wasn't I doing it?* The analyst was right—I could have already written the book. Instead I'd wasted almost two years of my life just yapping without acting. What was wrong with me? Was I in some sort of conflict about reaching my goal? It was then that I realized I'd been seeing a form of this same indecision in so many of the couples I was counseling, and I decided to tap into the powerful insights of conflict theory in order to come up with a more effective method for therapy.

Conflict theory is the core of most psychoanalytic treatment methods, so you could say that it has been around for ages. And if you referred to it as the "first talk therapy," you wouldn't be far off. Basically, conflict theory says that we all have inner conflicts left over from our childhoods—conflicts that have to do with unmet gratifications and desires—and that these conflicts may appear later in life as neurotic symptoms such as anxiety, depression, and even physical symptoms. This form of therapy was initially used to treat individuals. The thinking was that if the practicing psychoanalyst could uncover a patient's deepest conflicts, his or her symptoms would disappear. It was not thought to be a treatment for curing couples, even though it was believed that a cure in one partner might produce a cure in the relationship. In some cases this turned out to be true, but the prevailing belief is that the most effective way to treat a relationship is by seeing both partners together. Most couples therapists don't use conflict theory, but when I teamed key aspects of it with the couples theories I already knew, as I suspected, it proved to be the most powerful treatment formula I had ever observed in all my years of treating couples.

As I began to probe into the problems of the couples I was treating, I began to see that underlying those apparent troubles—fights about money, affairs, problems with in-laws, and so on—were deeper conflicts within each partner. The more I delved into these conflicts with couples, the clearer the pattern became; that so often couples had been brought together largely on the basis of a shared conflict, and now that shared conflict was pushing them apart.

Adding conflict theory to my treatment of couples made it easier for me to diffuse anger, to stop each partner from playing the blame game and help them learn to take responsibility for how each contributed to their relationship problems and thus reduce their relationship symptoms. Even those couples whose relationships were destined to end, usually because of a lack of motivation, were able to get unstuck and move on with their lives faster and with less animosity than I had been accustomed to witnessing. So, the first step in my work with couples is to fill them in about the role of master conflicts and their nature as quickly as possible and to start them on the process of thinking about what master conflict they may have. I will close this chapter by starting you on that process also.

KEY FACTS ABOUT MASTER CONFLICTS

As I said, most of us have a number of inner conflicts. So, how can we begin to determine which of these is playing the role of master conflict in our relationship? Your master conflict is the one that is the *most* important because it's usually

- *Beyond your awareness.* *Your master conflict is almost always repressed, or hidden in your unconscious. You may "know" about one side of your conflict, but not both sides, or what caused it.*

- *Deeply rooted in your past.* *Your master conflict started in your childhood.*

- *Always with you.* *Remember, because your master conflict is so deeply ingrained, it is nearly impossible to erase it completely.*

- *More powerful than any other conflict.* *Your master conflict dwarfs any other conflict you've got.*

- *Closely tied to your relationship problems.* *Your master conflict is more responsible for your relationship problems than any of your other conflicts.*

- *A factor in many areas of your life.* Your master conflict is not just a major factor in your relationships but may also underlie any problems you have experienced at work, with friends, and in other facets of life. Think of your problems as possible "symptoms" of your master conflict.

In the next several chapters, I will describe master conflicts in much more detail, introducing the most common ones I have seen in my practice, including many specific examples based on couples I have counseled, so that you will be able to get a good understanding of how they show up in relationships and how they lead to problems. As you read through those stories, you should be thinking about which of them resonate the most with you and are most similar to the story of your relationship. This will help you home in on which of them is probably at the core of your relationship troubles.

I'll also investigate where our master conflicts come from, describing how they usually stem from our early life experiences, and particularly from our family circumstances. I will then address the specific reasons why we generally hold onto our conflicts so tenaciously, which I think will help convince you that you should learn to manage your own conflict and also find a way to do so in your relationship.

Because most couples attribute their relationship problems not to a master conflict they share but rather to the one of three big issues—conflicts about sex, money, and in-laws—I will then explore how these problems are so often actually symptoms of a deeper, underlying master conflict rather than the root cause of the relationship crisis. I will then walk you through how to diagnose which master conflict may be causing the problems in your own relationship and how to manage it.

But first, in order to determine whether or not a master conflict may be the cause of your issues, you should take this short quiz, which I have found helps to pinpoint a master conflict that's gone out of control.

Master Conflict Impact-Assessment Quiz		
Questions	Yes	No
1. Have you been frustrated with your relationship for three months or longer?		
2. Are you often confused as to why you and your partner fight or argue?		
3. Do you and your partner argue about the same issue over and over?		
4. Do you and your partner argue with the same level of intensity over a variety of issues, even minor ones?		
5. Does your partner ever say or do things that don't make sense to you?		
6. Does your partner accuse you of the same things you accuse him or her of?		
7. Does it seem to you that you can never satisfy your partner?		
8. Does your partner show little or no interest in solving your relationship problems?		
9. When you get close to settling a problem does your partner sabotage the resolution or immediately create another problem?		
10. Have you been to counseling but nothing has changed?		

If you answered yes to five or more of these questions, then your relationship problems have the features that I've most often found indicate a master conflict at work. Take heart, because I have also found in my counseling that the knowledge of a master conflict is power, and that learning to better manage the frustrations it is causing is a wonderfully restorative process that has allowed many of the couples I've worked with to not only resolve their relationship crisis but achieve a new level of joy and appreciation of each other and of the value and deep satisfaction of their relationship.

2

THE MOST COMMON
MASTER CONFLICTS

There exists an obvious fact that seems utterly moral:
namely, that a man is always a prey to his truths.
—ALBERT CAMUS

The master conflicts I'll address here are the most common ones I have seen in my practice. I'll introduce seven of them first, because they are by far the most frequent, and then another four that are somewhat less common but also important, and I'll also describe what I learned about the origins of these conflicts for each partner in the couple. Reading these descriptions should help you begin to identify which inner conflicts you may have at play in your relationship and also start thinking about how these conflicts developed in you and your partner as you grew up. Keep in mind as you read these descriptions that most people have quite a few inner conflicts, and many of them may be playing roles in your life and in your relationship troubles—you may even have more than one of the conflicts I've listed. Ultimately, though, one particular conflict is usually causing the most trouble. So, as you read, begin to reflect on your own life and relationship and consider which of these you think are true for you. Later, you'll go through the process of zoning in more specifically on the one that is the key and is probably causing your worst relationship problems.

Keep in mind that this is not an exhaustive list; you and your partner may well have a conflict that is not described here—every relationship is, in the end, unique. I do describe several other master conflicts on pages 60–62, but perhaps reading about this most common set will help you to home in on the truth of your own situation more quickly. Some of my clients have made refinements to my diagnoses of the master conflicts that I thought best described their situation, and those refinements were vitally important for them. I do not at all want to encourage you to force your relationship into a box it doesn't fit into. My main mission is to provide you with a powerful way of diagnosing the specifics of your own relationship, and while you will almost certainly recognize your own relationship and its problems in many of the stories that follow, you should be careful to consider the differences as well. As you read, keep in mind particularly these key points about master conflicts:

- *Master conflicts vary in degree.* *Even if you think you've got one of the master conflicts you'll soon read about, it may not be as big a force in your life as it was for the couple I used to illustrate it. That's the good news. The bad news is, it may be bigger. For example, you may have your basic* closeness vs. distance *conflict, which causes you and your partner to struggle over the amount of emotional space that exists between the two of you. Maybe you both will have too many separate activities—or sex too infrequently. But another couple may suffer from an extreme version of this conflict and take turns actually staying and leaving one another. It's a variation on a theme.*

- ***You might recognize some of these conflicts but use other names to describe them.*** *For example, it might serve you better to call the* power vs. passivity *conflict the* parent-child combination, *or the* justice vs. injustice *conflict a* persecutor-victim *dynamic, or* success vs. sabotage *the* responsible vs. irresponsible *conflict. (Some of these have been used before by other therapists.) You may even come up with something entirely different that strikes your fancy. Whatever works! I chose labels that, in my experience, fit best with couples' histories, their problems or symptoms, and the direction that I think would have the strongest, most positive impact on them during treatment.*

- ***Some of the conflicts overlap.*** *Master conflicts have similar characteristics because they come from similar origins. That's to be expected. But I believe there's enough difference between them to merit distinction. Look for the one that best fits your situation.*

POWER VS. PASSIVITY

Power vs. passivity is perhaps the most common master conflict combination, and it is one of the most destructive. In this dynamic, both partners are conflicted about how much power and responsibility they should take in their relationship. Should the wife be in charge and run the show? Or should she be passive and let her husband take over? The partner who appears to be in charge usually needs the power yet also feels "burned out." The passive partner wants to be taken care of yet loathes being controlled; this partner also wants respect. Let's meet Marissa and Elliot.

Marissa, forty-three, enjoyed a thriving career as a corporate attorney. Dressed in a form-fitting navy blue business suit, she sat in my office with the nearly perfect posture you'd expect of a professional dancer. Looking me straight in the eye, Marissa said that she wanted Elliot, thirty-eight, her laid-back, less ambitious husband, to take more control of their family life and to be a stronger, more aggressive male role model for their eight- and ten-year-old boys. "He's got to step up—we have sons who look up to him. It's too much work for me to do everything," she said. At the same time, however, Marissa scolded and belittled Elliot at every turn, even in front of their children. Once, he tried to "step up," as Marissa put it, by deciding where the couple should live. What happened? Marissa shot down his idea calling it "incredibly stupid." Usually Marissa created so much fuss that Elliot would just give in and let her have her way. "What's the use of arguing with her? I'll never win," he said with a heavy sigh.

Marissa was in the thrall of the *power vs. passivity* conflict. If you asked her whether she truly wanted Elliot to be more powerful, she'd have said, "Yes, absolutely!" But she clearly demonstrated that *she* was the real power in the family and that she wasn't about to give up that power, despite her heavy workload.

Although Elliot complained about the way Marissa treated him, he played out his own conflict with power by making sure that he gave her enough reason to treat him like a child. How so? He'd lost more than one job because of laziness; he spent a great deal of time playing games on the internet; and he rarely did chores around the house even when asked. No doubt he would have gained greater self-confidence if he became more empowered, but he'd suffer the loss of the extended childhood his overindulgent parents helped to create. It was fitting that Elliot's usual uniform was a baseball cap, jeans, and sneakers.

Elliot was a passive organism, riding the great "surf of life." He rarely initiated anything, and even when he did, he left the burden of finishing it to someone else—usually Marissa. He thrived on getting others to cater to him, but he also had a deep feeling of incompetence and a gnawing irritation about being treated with disrespect. Elliot said in session one day, "I've never really achieved anything. Nobody really respects me, including my wife."

- *Marissa's conflict:* She wanted to be in charge, but she felt burdened by her responsibility.
- *Elliot's conflict:* He wanted to be treated with respect and have a say in family matters, but he wanted little responsibility, and he contributed very little.

Where Elliot's master conflict comes from

Elliot was excessively babied as a child, especially by his mother, and this pattern continued well into his thirties, as she lavished him with clothes, cars, trips, and all the cash he could spend without his ever having to work. His workaholic father was never around, but he made enough money for his wife to spoil Elliot. No surprise that young Elliot grew up to be high maintenance—a man who expected a lot from others and always tried to get away with doing as little as possible.

Where Marissa's master conflict comes from

Marissa's mother suffered from mental illness; she was in and out of hospitals for most of Marissa's childhood. To complicate matters, Marissa's father was a passive man, and he was overwhelmed by fatherhood, especially when his wife wasn't functioning. This was a perfect setup for Marissa—the eldest of four children—to serve as a substitute wife and mother. She developed a strong sense of responsibility, plus a fear that if she didn't take control, no one else would. After all, Marissa was accustomed to power. She made decisions that most kids her age would never be allowed to make, such as which bills should be paid first and whether or not her younger siblings should be taken to the doctor. This special power infused her with a strong sense of self-esteem and the belief that she could get things done. But it also tired her and placed more responsibility and stress on her than most children are equipped to handle. Though she was an excellent student, she was sick a lot, and even developed an ulcer at age fourteen. She also had little time for friends. Marrying Elliot enabled Marissa to replicate the hard life she had as a child.

GETTING YOUR NEEDS MET
VS. CARETAKING

In couples with the *getting your needs met vs. caretaking* master conflict, some sort of addiction—to alcohol, drugs, gambling, or sex—is often involved. A distinctive sign of this conflict is that one partner—usually a selfless type—focuses on the abusive or troubled mate to the detriment of his or her own needs. Let's take a look at the classic case, that of Michelle, fifty-three, and her alcoholic ex-husband, Tim, fifty-six.

When Michelle, a restaurant hostess, finally left her moody, hard-drinking husband, she swore to herself that she'd never become involved with another alcoholic. Sitting on the edge of her chair, Michelle looked me directly in the eyes and said with great determination in her voice, "I swear on my mother's grave, I'll never date a man who drinks too much again. I'm ashamed of myself for having lived like this for so long."

Making good on her promise, Michelle paid close attention to the drinking habits of her new suitors, breaking up with them at the slightest hint that they might have an alcohol problem. Despite her vigilance, however, Michelle was shocked and devastated to find that Rod, fifty-four, the man she had so carefully chosen to be her new mate, had a serious gambling problem. Her master conflict of *getting your needs met vs. caretaking* repeatedly steered her into relationships with addictive, abusive men who did everything in *their* power to satisfy their needs at her expense. Her master conflict was so strong that it had compelled her to give these men the best years of her life.

Crucially, these men shared her master conflict. In Michelle they found a caretaker, and yet they made it difficult—no, *impossible*—for her to actually take care of them. Tim rebelled against her pleas that he seek medical attention or join Alcoholics Anonymous (AA) by drinking even more and staying out even later at night. His health deteriorated and he lost more than one job. Rod refused treament as well and he ended up filing for bankruptcy. Because of Rod's debts, Michelle's car was repossessed in the middle of the night. To understand more about the nature of this conflict and where it might come from, let's take a closer look at Michelle and Tim.

- *Michelle's conflict:* She wanted to get her needs met, but she didn't feel as if she deserved the attention. Michelle was a caretaker who put most of her effort into nurturing needy men who couldn't or wouldn't meet her needs.
- *Tim's conflict:* He wanted to be taken care of, but he blocked everybody, especially Michelle, from helping him—his was a "slow suicide."

Where Michelle's master conflict comes from

Michelle's mother was jealous of her daughter's great looks and her close relationship with her father, who was a severe alcoholic. Throughout Michelle's childhood, her mother was verbally and emotionally abusive, and she was especially critical of Michelle's appearance because of her own insecurities. Michelle tried hard to stay connected to her dad—specifically by never making a mistake in his presence and by tolerating his gruff personality. When he was stranded at his favorite neighborhood bar, she would bring him home and put him to bed. Michelle had hoped this caretaking would endear her to him, but he rarely remembered the nights before his drunken binges. Michelle also took great pains to make her mother like her, but this never worked. Michelle's parents finally ended their miserable marriage when she was eighteen. Michelle immediately married Tim and never saw her mother again, though when she died, a few years later, Michelle took the high road and attended the funeral. Easy to see how Michelle learned to be a chronic caretaker and pleaser. By marrying Tim, she was able to continue to put another person's needs ahead of her own, no matter how miserable it made her.

Where Tim's master conflict comes from

Poor Tim didn't have a chance. He came from a long line of alcoholics—father, mother, and both grandfathers were heavy drinkers. Every night, Tim would make dinner for his little brother, because his parents would routinely stop at the neighborhood bar after work, get drunk, and come home after midnight. Tim tried to stay away from the booze, but as work and life pressures mounted, he self-medicated with alcohol. And in her way Michelle was a good fit for him.

CLOSENESS VS. DISTANCE

We all regulate closeness and distance, though how we do so depends on our tolerance for intimacy. While some people can't go out for a cheeseburger without their partner, others feel suffocated if they don't have enough alone time. I'll never forget the time I asked a good friend, who lived nearby, if he could grab a quick bite to eat with me, because I had something important to discuss with him. "Shouldn't you ask your wife if you can go?" he asked. But my wife handled distance easily; she would probably shoot me a funny look if I asked permission for something like this. That was not true for my friend and his wife, though; they always checked with each other.

Some people might say that my friend and his wife were overly dependent: "joined at the hip." But as long as partners agree on the amount of closeness and distance, it doesn't matter what the rest of us think. It's the couples who can't decide how much closeness or distance they want who have a problem. They will often shift back and forth between periods of wanting more closeness and times when they want more distance, and they may often be out of sync in their desires. Such constant balancing is a tricky and tiresome task. Consider the case of Jeremy, twenty-eight, and Belinda, twenty-six, a young couple whose master conflict of *closeness vs. distance* almost landed them in divorce court.

They struggled mightily with closeness and distance. Every time one would come in close, the other would find a way to create more distance. Every time one would be too distant, the other would complain. The techniques both partners used to maintain their conflict ranged from starting fights to disappearing for a stretch of time. It got to the point that sleeping in the same bed was too close for them—a very bad sign for such a young couple. Let's listen in on a conversation they had during a session, which reveals these dynamics; notice that each takes little responsibility for their own personal conflict about relationship space.

> **Belinda:** I can't believe you went running when you knew I wanted you to watch a movie with me.
>
> **Jeremy:** Why should I watch a movie with you? You've been angry with me all day, and I don't even know why. I'd rather go for a stress-free run.
>
> **Belinda:** *(Sarcastically)* Yeah, you never contribute to our problems, do you?
>
> **Jeremy:** Are you kidding? When we were at the restaurant having a nice lunch, you started a fight with me over nothing. I want to be close to you, but it's like hanging out with an angry boss—I'm always doing something wrong.
>
> **Belinda:** First of all, it wasn't "over nothing." You weren't listening to me when I was talking. You were in outer space.

Jeremy: I was listening. I only stopped listening when you got
angry.

My take on the situation, based on my observations of him
over time, was that Jeremy did probably act as if he was in "outer
space" at the restaurant. This was his way of unconsciously creating
space in an intimate setting. When Belinda caught Jeremy distanc-
ing, instead of dealing with it in a way that could maintain closeness, she created more space with her anger, which gave Jeremy
the opportunity to get mad and run away from her at movie time.
Both partners claimed that they desperately wanted to be close and
to stop their bickering. But the reality is that they couldn't seem
to be in the same place at the same time and get along. Such is the
closeness vs. distance master conflict.

- *Belinda's conflict:* She wanted to be in a close, passionate
  relationship, but she was terrified of suffering loss.
- *Jeremy's conflict:* He desperately wanted to form his own
  family and create his own security and stability. But he too
  was so afraid of being abandoned that he couldn't fully
  commit to anyone, especially someone he loved as much
  as Belinda.

Where Jeremy's master conflict comes from

Jeremy came from what I call a splintered home. He had a distant
relationship with his father, and his mother had moved in and out
of his life. To add to his insecurity, two ex-fiancées left him for
other men. He wanted closeness, but closeness scared him—and
posed too much risk.

Where Belinda's master conflict comes from

Belinda's parents were divorced when she was young. Devastated by the split, she developed an extremely close relationship with her father, whom she saw as the victim in the marriage. The two were inseparable for the next six years, until her father eventually remarried. Once again, Belinda was traumatized. Somewhat like Jeremy, she said she was so afraid of loss that she decided not to get close to another man again. Belinda added to her conflict by loving men who didn't love her back. Just like Jeremy, she too craved closeness but also feared it.

CONFORMITY VS. REBELLION

The *conformity vs. rebellion* conflict is one of the more common master conflicts. In this dynamic, one side of you wants to conform to or fall in line with what others want you to do or be. But the more mischievous side of you is a rebel. If it's black, then you say it's blue. If it's blue, then you say it's black. The rebellion started in your family of origin. Where else? And it lives on in your present relationship. While conforming brings lots of positive reinforcement from others, rebellion causes you to suffer the consequences. If you upset somebody, the person may let you know about it in a way that really hurts. Samantha (Sam as she liked to be called), twenty-seven, was a beauty, but she covered up her great looks by wearing little if any makeup, large round glasses, and an assortment of baggy sweat suits. Ironically, she worked as a bartender at a dive bar, and it was only at work that she flaunted her good looks and sexuality.

Sam was threatening to divorce Vince, her twenty-nine-year-old husband. Why? Vince was supportive and "turned on" by her flirtatious behavior at work, but he kept close watch over her activities. "Even though he got off on my teasing other men, he is like a Nazi," she said. "He goes to my bar and he gives me hell if he thinks I'm getting too close with any of the customers. One night, he thought a customer got too fresh with me while I was sitting in for a waitress. So what did the idiot do? He started a fight! Can you believe it? I have bouncers for that. I was so embarrassed! The bouncers had to throw Vince and the customer out of the bar. Sometimes I'd worry so much about doing something that would piss Vince off that I'd lose my concentration. I was looking at him more than at the customers."

Furious with Vince, Sam reacted the best way she knew how—by rebelling against her husband. She began by flirting even more with the customers.

It was Vince's worst nightmare, and he freaked out. Yet he wanted the marriage to survive. Question: If Vince was so worried about his wife's activities, why was he okay with her working at a honky-tonk to begin with? Answer: This decision fit in with Vince's dual persona. He was a strong family man, but he also had some of the rebel in him. He was a professional musician, playing bass in a rock band, and he loved the rebellious spirit of rock. Like his wife, Vince was a mix of conservative and bohemian—a conformer and a rebel.

- *Samantha's conflict:* Sam wanted to conform to the norms of polite society. In fact, she liked the idea of being a mother and housewife. But she also was a rebel, one who craved the freedom to do whatever she wanted, including working in a seedy bar.

- *Vince's conflict:* Vince was also half conservative and half bohemian. He liked the idea of being married, having kids, and living in the suburbs. But, though he looked every inch the hippie and was turned on by his wife's adventurous side, he just couldn't seem to control her "wild child."

Where Samantha's master conflict comes from

This one you can see a mile away—the duality is that clear. Sam grew up in a very strict home. Her father, a police officer, was unbearably controlling and held her to an almost impossibly high standard. Her mother was passive and content to let her husband be the boss. Sam's conformity conflict emerged when she was in junior high; she set out to be a real role model by becoming a straight-A student, cheerleader, and member of the student council. But she also drank, experimented with drugs, and had sex early and often. "My parents didn't know what I was doing in my spare time," she said. "They really didn't know me, because even back then I led a double life."

Where Vince's master conflict comes from

Vince's father was a painter and sculptor, but oddly enough, he was also an authoritarian conservative who ran his home with an iron fist. As a result, Vince grew up confused as to whether he should be a conforming conservative or a rebellious hippie. He said that at different times in his life he tried to choose between the two but didn't feel comfortable on either side. In fact, he jokingly referred to himself as a "hybrid." Vince's mother was passive and, like Sam's mother, she let her husband take charge at home.

JUSTICE VS. INJUSTICE

This is perhaps the most interesting of all the master conflicts. It's one in which the two partners share a strong sense of fairness and a heightened sensitivity to injustice. I originally thought of this as a *trust vs. distrust* conflict, but the righteous, indignant reactions that are distinctive signs of this conflict, along with each partner's history of unfairness in his or her family of origin, convinced me to see it as a conflict about justice. Framing the problem this way also seemed to have a greater impact on the couples in the grip of this conflict.

Most people with a *justice vs. injustice* master conflict have good hearts. But they can become very angry and indignant when they feel they're wronged. That's one side of the conflict. The other side is that these same people miraculously get themselves into situations that guarantee injustice and continuous struggle. In extreme cases, they see injustice where it really doesn't exist. Simply put, they "want and don't want" justice—they can't decide between the two.

Longtime cohabitants Gerry and Marlene confessed their love for each other but fought constantly and couldn't figure out why. Even worse, most of their fights were over minor issues, such as an untimely response to a telephone call. Two nice people . . . one big mess. Why?

Gerry was a private man who kept his thoughts and feelings close to the vest. Marlene liked openness. She enjoyed calling Gerry at work to chat; she wanted to know where he was at all times; and she believed that a couple shouldn't keep secrets from each other. This was way too close for Gerry—he felt as if he were living inside an MRI machine, but if he didn't answer his cell phone—which he usually didn't at work—Marlene would become angry, hurt, and suspicious. She would then launch an investigation into what he'd been doing that Sherlock Holmes would envy. And Gerry would, of course, object to her intrusiveness, calling it "ridiculous and unjustified." "It's unfair for him to block me out of his life," Marlene said one day in a session. "What kind of man does that?" The more the couple squabbled, the longer Gerry put off marriage. "No way am I going to marry you and start a family while we're fighting like this," he said. Having lived with Gerry for several years, Marlene felt that his putting off the marriage was unfair—that he might be stringing her along with no intention of ever marrying. Around and around they went.

At any given moment, either Gerry or Marlene might start the cycle of injustice. Sometimes Gerry would unconsciously bait Marlene into investigating him. It took him a long time to admit it, but his favorite technique was to give her partial information, which heightened her anxiety and suspicion. Marlene shared the following example of their fight over Jane, Gerry's former law partner. Marlene was always jealous of Jane, and she was convinced that Gerry was romantically interested in her. Although Jane had long been a source of trouble for the couple, there was never any solid evidence that she and Gerry had anything more than a professional relationship. Let's listen:

Marlene: I heard Jane is back in town.
Gerry: Yeah.
Marlene: Have you seen her?
Gerry: Yeah.
Marlene: Where?

Gerry: I saw her yesterday but I didn't get a chance to talk to her much.

Marlene: (*Smirking*) Well, I heard that there was a party at the office and that's where you saw her.

Gerry: Oh yeah. I forgot.

Marlene: (*Angry*) You forgot to tell me you saw her at your office party?

Gerry: It's no big deal.

Marlene: You always do this. Why do you lie?

Gerry: I didn't lie. I didn't think the details were important.

For her part, Marlene could manufacture a problem that didn't exist, creating an injustice in her mind and then feeling victimized. She would then unjustly accuse Gerry of a transgression, and he would take the bait and react with angry indignation. The following exchange between them clearly demonstrates this dynamic.

Gerry: I hate it when you call me at work to start a fight. Yesterday you called three times and accused me of trying to arrange a secret meeting with Jane. I think you're crazy. I think you need medication.

Marlene: Well, you usually come home around six o'clock from work, and this time you showed up at seven thirty. How do I know where you were? What I *do* know is that Jane's back in town.

Gerry: But I've told you a thousand times that I've never had any interest in her. She was just my partner.

Marlene: You worked closely with her.

Gerry: (*Sarcastic*) Yeah. She was my partner. We worked in a small law office together.

Marlene: What about the time you went to a conference together? That was over the top.

Gerry: *(With frustration)* What do you mean? We sometimes have to go to conferences together. Our legal secretary went with us. This is crazy. I can't take it anymore!

- *Marlene's conflict:* She longed for a close, unconditionally loving relationship, but she was also attracted to injustice, having grown up in a family that valued males more than females.
- *Gerry's conflict:* He wanted to avoid being controlled—he couldn't take the injustice of it. But he unconsciously sought injustice, especially in his relationships. Like a superhero, he needed to be battling injustices.

Where Gerry's master conflict comes from

Gerry's described his father as an "extremely controlling" man who had lots of rules and always had to have his way.

Gerry grew up fearing his dad to the point where he had frequent fantasies about running away from home. But he stayed put until he left for college, because he didn't want to leave his mother and siblings.

Gerry wanted justice, so why did he seek injustice as well? For two reasons: First, it was familiar to him. Second, he could fight against it and release his lingering anger at his father.

Where Marlene's master conflict comes from

Marlene was of Italian descent on her mother's side, and her mother was "old-school Italian." She said that this meant that the rules for men and women were different in her family—though Marlene was under tight control and scrutiny, her brothers were allowed to do whatever they pleased. This really angered Marlene, who called the different rules "completely unfair." She constantly fought with her mother for approval and freedom, but she could never win. As time went on, Marlene became filled with a sense of injustice. In adulthood, she fought long and hard against it, especially in her relationships with men.

SUCCESS VS. SABOTAGE
(BIG VS. SMALL)

In the *success vs. sabotage* master conflict, generally both partners have plenty of potential to succeed professionally, but they find ways to limit their achievements. While they don't always completely fail, they somehow seem to block themselves from reaching their goals. I also refer to this as the *big vs. small* master conflict because these people are afraid to be big and successful yet also fear being small and a failure. To balance this conflict, they often aim for semisuccess, essentially driving through life with the brakes on. Let's see how Shari and Paul dealt with this master conflict.

Shari, forty-three, wore an angry scowl on her face as she stomped into my office. Her husband, Paul, forty-six, a restaurant manager, stared down at his shoes, waiting for the deluge. And it came. "I'm so sick of Paul's crap," Shari yelled. "He's not living up to his responsibilities. I want to move to a bigger home. I really feel ripped off; I married a loser." Paul sheepishly replied, "I'd love to live in a better neighborhood, but we just don't make enough money. We're struggling to pay our current mortgage as it is. I don't see it happening unless we win the lottery."

At face value, this looked simple: a wife who was deeply hurt and angry with her husband's inability to meet her standards. But a closer look revealed that a shared master conflict of *success vs. sabotage* was the culprit. While watching them in action, notice that they want the same things in life, but instead of resolving their own personal conflicts about success, they make excuses and blame each other for their unfulfilled dreams.

Dr. B.: Shari, you're really mad.

Shari: *(Furious)* Like I said, I feel cheated. I want a better life for us and our daughter, but Paul can't—or won't—make it happen. For God's sake, you have an MBA, Paul! Why are you working in that lousy-paying restaurant job, anyway? I thought you were going to be somebody.

Paul: *(Frustrated)* Not every MBA becomes a millionaire. I think it's unfair of you to expect me to pull off a financial miracle. I feel like I've done okay for the family to this point. If you're so unhappy, why don't you go back to work? You've got a master's degree in special education.

Shari: So why did you tell me I could stay home and raise children? I was working full-time when we met. I had a stable career as a teacher. Why did you mislead me?

Paul: I am supporting the family, thank you. I didn't know you wanted to be supported like a movie star.

Shari: I don't want to be supported lavishly. I want what everybody else wants for their family: a nice house in a nice neighborhood, and the best education I can get for my kid. Is that too much to ask from a guy with an advanced degree? Besides, aren't you the one who said, "An MBA is the key to success?" Tell Dr. Betchen how many of your former classmates manage a restaurant.

Dr. B.: Shari, what do you think about Paul's suggestion that you go back to work?

Paul: Yeah. You've got a solid teaching background. Don't you want to use it?

Shari: Now you want me to use it; before, you wanted me to forget about it. What about you? What's your goal? To be the most overeducated restaurant manager in the country?

- *Shari's conflict:* Part of her demanded to be successful, but the other side of her blocked her from reaching her goals.
- *Paul's conflict:* He wanted to achieve great success, but, like Shari, another side of him wanted to fail. Giving up was easy for Paul. As he once said to me with a sarcastic chuckle, "What's the use of trying? No matter what I accomplish, nobody seems to care. Now I don't give a shit."

Where Paul's master conflict comes from

Paul's parents showed very little interest in him. His father was a very critical man who never seemed to be impressed with anything or anybody. Even when Paul accomplished a great feat and completed his MBA, his father decided not to attend the graduation because he had a tee time at a famous golf course. Paul's mother, dependent and passive, rarely defied her husband so she missed the graduation ceremony as well. Academically gifted, Paul dreamed upon entering graduate school of one day becoming the CEO of a major company. But after completing his graduate degree he went into an inexplicable emotional slump and returned to the restaurant where he worked during his undergraduate days. Rather than be proud of his academic accomplishments, Paul felt that he had little to offer and harbored anger at his parents for not reinforcing any achievements he did make.

Where Shari's master conflict comes from

Shari's father was verbally abusive, losing his temper over nothing. Shari's mother was passive; Shari believed that her mother simply tried to protect herself from her husband's temper and was probably glad that he wasn't picking on her. Shari was an angry woman, and because she suffered emotional abuse as a child, she developed a strong sense of entitlement. She also had no clear concept of how to reach her goals, which led her to behave aggressively.

SPECIALNESS VS. ORDINARINESS

In this master conflict, each partner struggles between being ordinary versus being someone special. They see themselves as plain, ordinary folk no matter how accomplished they are . . . and they hate it. Sadly, to compensate for this ordinariness, they feel the need to make themselves feel special in some way as often as they can. This usually includes showering themselves with material gifts and constantly looking to others to validate them. If they do deprive themselves of something, it may last for only a brief period, because the anxiety of being ordinary is too much; they must recapture that special feeling. People with this master conflict surround themselves with those who make them feel special, but because they are in conflict, they often minimize the specialness given to them. Consider the story of a forty-six-year-old lawyer and her forty-eight-year-old husband, who had a whopper of a *specialness vs. ordinariness* master conflict.

Sophia was a smart, successful woman; her husband, Nicholas, was equally smart and successful, but mild-mannered. They had three children and they seemed to have it all, yet Sophia wasn't satisfied with her life, so she continuously tried to realize whatever fantasy popped into her mind. It's easy to call Sophia self-centered and insatiable—and there would be some truth to that. But it wouldn't really capture her precise dilemma. In treatment, she often reported having done something new and exciting—she was always searching for more ways to enrich her already super-enriched life. But she wasn't selfish; she was in deep conflict. Sophia did everything she could to avoid being ordinary. Her frequent trips to Europe and her excessive spending habits were the medications she used to protect herself from having to deal with being ordinary. Her dark, exotic looks and quick wit were easy lures for most men—although she somehow managed to remain loyal to her husband. But if Sophia had so much ability to keep herself feeling special, why would she need therapy? There was another side to Sophia: She wanted to settle down and be fulfilled as a wife and mother. She also was tired of the frenetic pace she'd set for herself—a standard that was nearly impossible to maintain over time. And, yes . . . she did suffer some guilt about her behavior.

Sophia's life was exhausting. She tried to solve her master conflict by stopping her behavior cold turkey, but the longest she could last was about three months. In crisis, she would start another project or buy something extravagant. But only by resolving her conflict psychologically would she ever find true relief. To do this, she had to accept the fact that she was special in her own distinct way, but accept her limitations as well. No small feat.

Nicholas was a nice guy, and Sophia knew it. But it didn't help that he had the same conflict. Nicholas fed his own need to feel special by getting so involved with his community volunteer activities, sports, and computer projects that he sometimes forgot he was married. Sophia was able to get away with her behavior because her husband simply wasn't paying attention—a neglect that fueled Sophia's need to feel special. Nicholas then became just another guy to Sophia—nobody special.

- *Sophia's conflict:* She wanted desperately to maintain the specialness to which she'd grown accustomed. But she also wanted to "slow down," live a more conventional lifestyle, and become a better wife and mother.
- *Nicholas's conflict:* He felt special when he was participating in the activities that brought him personal and professional satisfaction and success. Avoiding interaction with his wife, especially anything negative, allowed him to feel secure and stable. But his distance greatly detracted from his specialness, particularly in his wife's eyes. It also kept him out of touch with her needs, putting himself at risk for loss.

Where Nicholas's master conflict comes from

Nicholas grew up in a family that exhibited poor communication skills and avoided negativity at all costs—the primary reason he's a bad communicator today. For example, if anything bad or traumatic happened to a family member, it wasn't discussed. No one ever released anger either. Family members went about their business no matter what was happening. When his mother was diagnosed with breast cancer, Nicholas, twelve at the time, knew something was wrong but was never told—and didn't ask.

Both of Nicholas's parents were quiet, conservative, and cordial. He doesn't recall their ever arguing. This would have been okay if they at least discussed serious issues, such as his mother's illness or the failure of his father's automobile business, which left the family in a temporary financial crisis, but they didn't. Nicholas and his siblings learned to fill their time with personal projects—mostly sports and computer-related activities. Nicholas felt special because he excelled in these areas, and it paid off for him when he eventually landed a prestigious, high-paying job in his field. But he also paid a price: poor communication and a lack of connection to his wife and children.

Where Sophia's master conflict comes from

Sophia was her father's favorite child. He saw her vast potential, so he closely guided her life and often treated her to trips to a museum or the opera. While Sophia had a decent relationship with her mother, the strong father-daughter connection dominated, laying the groundwork for the development of her master conflict. Sophia's father was an overachiever who delighted in his daughter's successes. But while her achievements pleased him and met most of her own aspirations, she had little left for anyone else in her life, and this cost her.

If you couldn't see any of those seven most common master conflicts in yourself and your relationship, then it may be that one of the four described below will resonate with you. But remember that it is possible none of these conflicts perfectly captures the struggle that you and your partner may be locked in either. As I said, each relationship is ultimately unique, and as common as these issues are for couples, yours may well be different.

ADEQUACY VS. INADEQUACY

This master conflict is similar to *success vs. sabotage*, the difference being that couples who suffer from *adequacy vs. inadequacy* may be successful—some extremely so. Yet they don't feel that way because of their internal conflict. There may not even be much sabotaging going on, just some confusion about how they should allow themselves to feel about their accomplishments. It might not sound so bad to you, but couples with this conflict shift back and forth by making themselves and each other feel strong and confident, and then weak and helpless. When both partners support each other, life may be peachy. But this doesn't last too long, and soon they find a way to feel bad. Not only do they underestimate the amount of support they give to each other but they also underestimate how impotent they make each other feel. Ken, thirty-four, an anesthesiologist, and Molly, thirty-one, a part-time hairdresser, are a great example of this master conflict.

Molly and Ken came to therapy because they were arguing about money, specifically Molly's insistence that Ken earn more so they could enroll their two sons in an expensive private school. "They need better educations," she said. "I want to give them an edge. Ken's capable of making more money but he won't." Ken responded with anger. "We have a great school system in our town. I just don't get her. It's always something else. She's never satisfied."

During therapy, Ken was indeed angry, and Molly did act spoiled. But what really intrigued me was that they had such a seemingly enviable life. Something didn't add up. Sure, maybe Ken could have tacked on another $100,000 to his already huge salary by moonlighting at another hospital, but it seemed to me that both mates were overreacting to each other. What did I learn?

Eventually I realized that both Ken and Molly continually shifted between feeling good about themselves and each other and tearing each other down. Their *adequacy vs. inadequacy* conflict was tricky to pick up on, because they shrouded their problems in money issues. For example, Molly, feeling insecure about her looks as well as her failure to achieve more in her career, would focus on Ken's income and the flaws in her children's schooling. A frustrated Ken wanted to make his wife happy. But realizing that nothing he tried really worked—that he was "helpless"—he became angry and even less productive. That's the inadequate side. On the other hand, both recognized that they were smart; each admired the other—as they should.

- *Ken's conflict:* He wanted to feel adequate and admired by his wife. Yet, in marrying Molly, he chose a woman who, because she was never satisfied with herself or with him, enabled him to feel inadequate.

- *Molly's conflict:* Like Ken, Molly wanted to feel good about herself. But she consistently found ways to feel inadequate. By blaming Ken for his failure to fulfill all her heart's desires, Molly could avoid dealing with her own deep inadequacy.

Where Ken's master conflict comes from

Ken's father was a gambler who squandered the family's money. He eventually divorced Ken's mother for another woman, leaving the family penniless. Ken had always been very disappointed in his father. Several times he tried to help him overcome his addiction, but his father was too sick to change. As he did with his father, Ken tried and tried to please Molly, but nothing worked. The result? Anger, frustration, sadness, and a feeling of helplessness and inadequacy.

Where Molly's master conflict comes from

As a child Molly was doted upon. She admitted that she developed a sense of entitlement, as well as a poor work ethic; if something didn't come fast and easy, she became frustrated and gave up. In treatment, Molly found that her impulsive, demanding behavior, a result of her parents' overindulgences, never allowed her to accomplish much on her own (or learn to work toward her goals). Replicating the relationship she had with her parents, Molly looked to Ken to meet her demands, some of which were irrational. When he failed, her inadequacy kicked in because she knew she couldn't meet her needs on her own. Molly's answer to this problem was to increase the pressure on Ken to meet her needs, causing his anger and feelings of helplessness and inadequacy to rear up.

CONTROL VS. CHAOS
(CONTROL VS. OUT OF CONTROL)

Some people are conflicted about being in control—part of them wants control and stability and will do everything in their power to get it; the other part of them craves the excitement of chaos. People with this master conflict may never get too close to anybody or "tied down." It's not unusual for them to have been in hundreds of relationships and to have slept with as many partners. People like this usually struggle with commitment. But what distinguishes them from someone with a *commitment vs. freedom* conflict is the drama or chaos in the situation—the other side of their conflict. In other words, someone with a *control vs. chaos* master conflict desperately wants to call the shots—to be the decision maker in the relationship—but also has a need to be out of control. These people show this side of the conflict by falling hard for someone who is completely out of control. The ongoing struggle to gain and lose control is exhilarating yet chaotic. Sometimes it can even be dangerous; indeed, it's different from the *risk vs. security* conflict in that it usually features more drama.

Todd, forty-two, had it all: great looks, a successful career, a beautiful condo, a vacation home in the Caribbean, fancy cars, and all the spare cash he could spend. He also was a self-proclaimed "stud," having slept with hundreds of women.

If Todd had it all, why would he need to see me? Well, Todd was in crisis. He'd finally gotten hooked on a woman and was squirming like a fish on a line. Who was this woman and what was so special about her? Ginny was a thirty-four-year-old spitfire. Out of all the women Todd had or could have, why did she

51

command his fanatical interest? How did she seize Todd's control? How could Ginny make him do things that even he couldn't believe were possible? First, Ginny, a radiology technician, was both controlling and demanding of Todd as no other woman had been. She *ordered* him to meet her every need. This included paying her bills and lavishing her with gifts. She also continued to see and sleep with previous boyfriends. If Todd refused her demands or protested her behavior, she could become violent. For example, one evening Todd threatened to stop paying some of her expenses if she didn't stop sleeping around and Ginny attacked him with a frying pan. Yes, Ginny was in control of a controlling person—quite a feat!

As crazy as this couple may seem, their master conflicts matched up beautifully. When Todd attempted to control the relationship, Ginny would prevent him from doing so by acting out of control. When Ginny was in control, Todd might threaten to abandon her or cut her off financially—this would then flip her out-of-control switch. These two were like a pair of pistons that could never be in the same place at the same time. Both were conflicted about being in control and needed each other to maintain their *control vs. chaos* master conflict.

- *Ginny's conflict:* On one level she wanted control and stability. But the other side of her wanted freedom and the excitement of being out of control.
- *Todd's conflict:* He wanted control and stability, but he also enjoyed the thrill of a chaotic lifestyle—infidelity and wild sex.

Where Todd's master conflict comes from

Todd's family of origin was about both control and chaos. Although his parents had what appeared to be a stable marriage—they were together until his mother died of complications from diabetes at sixty-one—they constantly cheated on each other throughout their entire forty-year relationship. Todd remembers catching each of them with other people several times. He saw his father at a restaurant with a woman and once found his mother kissing a man in a parked car outside a bowling alley. "It was weird, but it became a way of life, so I got used to it," Todd said.

Where Ginny's master conflict comes from

Ginny grew up in an extremely rigid, religious family. "There were rules about rules," she said. "I couldn't stand it. But if I didn't follow them, I was punished. My parents didn't speak to me for almost a year after I broke up with a boy who was a member of our church. To this day, I still don't like them." Ginny said she couldn't be herself until she moved out of her parents' house, and when she finally did, she really "cut loose."

LEGITIMACY VS. ILLEGITIMACY

If you were adopted, orphaned, treated in childhood as if you didn't measure up—if you were made to feel "less than" in some way—you may have the *legitimacy vs. illegitimacy* master conflict. It doesn't matter much if, in the end, you were adopted by a set of wonderful parents, or were taken in by a loving aunt and uncle.

No, the odds are that you'll still question your own legitimacy—your value as a human being. In a nutshell, you'll question whether you truly "belong" or that you're an "imposter." When out of control, this can be an enormously painful conflict. People with it never seem to feel comfortable with themselves or where they are. To compensate, they often overwork to prove their value to whoever looks after them. But they also may sabotage their new home, because deep down they feel they don't deserve to be loved—they feel illegitimate.

This master conflict is somewhat similar to the *acceptance vs. rejection* conflict. What differentiates the two? Those who suffer from the *legitimacy vs. illegitimacy* conflict struggle specifically with feeling like a fake or an imposter. That's the major difference. Let's see this master conflict in action.

Carol, thirty-three, was pretty and bright. Yet she didn't feel like much on the inside. Her husband, George, thirty-four, worshipped her but couldn't win her approval. She harped on him constantly, belittled his manhood, and rarely slept with him. Carol admitted that most women would "kill" to have George, who came from a wealthy family—a family she loved, because they treated her as if she were their own daughter. But Carol was fighting an invisible force that kept telling her to keep George away.

Not surprisingly, George was deeply hurt and frustrated. He'd tried to please Carol in every way. He'd even given up hobbies and friendships to win her acceptance. George was so afraid of not having his wife's approval that he didn't even realize how much of himself he had been sacrificing. Though it was clear to his friends and siblings that he was never going to be good enough for his wife, he maintained that she was his superior and worthy of his attempts to satisfy her. At one point George excused Carol for chastising him by claiming that she was only trying to "make him a better man."

- *Carol's conflict:* Carol wanted to be in a solid marriage and to be part of a loving family. She got all this with George. But because she felt illegitimate—like an outsider—she was always on the verge of destroying their relationship.
- *George's conflict:* George wanted to be loved and respected by his wife, Carol. But he married a woman who repeatedly questioned his legitimacy as a real man—as his father had done in the workplace.

Where Carol's master conflict comes from

Carol was adopted as an infant. Her adoptive parents divorced when she was only eight and she lived with her mother, who eventually remarried, to a man whom Carol calls "a mean guy." Once she left for college she never returned home, because she didn't feel wanted. Carol was angry with both her adoptive and biological parents. It makes sense that she would want a nice family yet not feel comfortable in creating one.

Where George's master conflict comes from

George grew up in the shadow of a successful but highly critical father, who always tried to emasculate him. The result? George never felt good enough in his dad's eyes, and when there was talk about his taking over the family masonry business, his dad let George know that he was a fraud—not man enough to do the job. Though George knew he had talent, his insecurity got the best of him, and he began to think that his father might be right. Although not adopted or orphaned, George still questioned his own legitimacy, and the way Carol treated him fed into his problem.

PERSON VS. OBJECT

Partners with the *person vs. object* master conflict treat themselves and each other as objects, more like chess pieces to be manipulated and maneuvered than like human beings. While both partners with this conflict want to be treated as people, not objects, they put themselves in a position to be treated otherwise, and a cycle of mutual disrespect is the result. Here's a brief example of how this works: Trey, an airline pilot, consistently spoke to his wife, Joyce, as if she were a sexual object. For example, instead of respectfully complimenting her on her new dress, Trey would say something like "Oh, you've got a new dress. You must want it really bad tonight." While most of Trey's comments were insulting, instead of getting angry and putting an end to his behavior, Joyce would reinforce it by responding with something like "That's right. Can you handle it, big boy?" Sometimes Joyce would start the process by referring to Trey as a sexual object, to which Trey would respond in kind. What's most interesting about this dynamic is that all the while it's happening, one or both partners complain about being mistreated. It's common for couples to use sex to support their *person vs. object* master conflict, but they can use other avenues of support as well. Let's take a look at a couple that typifies what I mean.

Kristen, a thirty-two-year-old, and her husband, Kirk, thirty-seven, treated themselves and each other as objects, or "performance robots"; they didn't know any other way to be. Their standards for behavior were almost unattainable. Kristen was dissatisfied with Kirk's low six-figure salary. She complained that as an orthodontist he should have been making almost double the amount. What's more, she didn't want him to express anger or complain about anything related to their marriage, and she disapproved whenever he tried to relax because she believed there were always household chores that needed attention. Kristen was rarely affectionate to Kirk and had sex with him only if he met her standards. Kirk reinforced Kristen's robotic treatment of him by trying to meet her unrealistic and inhuman requirements without complaint. But this doesn't mean that he let Kristen off the hook. Kirk demanded that she continue to be a superstar as well. He made it known that he wanted Kristen to maintain her high six-figure salary and her beauty as well. If she gained a pound or two he'd be quick to tell her. Not that Kristen needed him to be hard on her—she was tough enough on herself—but he did help to reinforce her perfectionism.

- *Kristen's conflict:* She wanted to be human—to be loved unconditionally. But she was raised like an object. Like Kirk, she had difficulty loving and being loved.
- *Kirk's conflict:* He wanted to feel human emotions—and to express himself and live his life without fear. But he was also raised as an agreeable robot, and as a result he felt most secure this way.

Where Kirk's master conflict comes from

Kirk grew up hiding from his mother, who had an unpredictable temper. He hid a lot in his room, sometimes shaking in his closet while she had a fit.

It's easy to see how Kirk evolved into a perfect robot as opposed to a human being with passion and emotions. In his family of origin, passion and emotion were dangerous qualities to have.

Where Kristen's master conflict comes from

When Kristen was eleven, her parents divorced. Her mother moved away and remarried; Kristen described her as "selfish," and they had no contact for many years. Kristen lived with her father, who soon married another selfish woman. But Kristen's stepmother also was demanding and manipulative—to the point where everything was conditional with her. "Whenever I disappointed her, she'd shun me for weeks," Kristen said.

Kristen's father, fearing he would lose another partner, supported his new wife in every disagreement she had with Kristen. This left Kristen with no alternative; she *had* to please her stepmother, because life was unbearable if she didn't. So she become an agreeable Barbie doll—beautiful, flawless, and without an independent thought or feeling, especially a controversial one. After graduating from a prestigious college and earning a master's degree in hospital administration, she landed a plum position with a six-figure salary. She was perfect! But no matter what she accomplished, Kristen was never able to please her stepmother, so she kept working at it. In other words, she was treated as an object rather than a person. She wanted to be human, but because she had never been treated as one, she began to believe she was an object.

After reading about all these conflicts, you may be getting a sense of a set of them that you think are at play in your own life and relationship. In order to begin the process of homing in on which of these you may need to focus on, I suggest that you review the conflicts below (listed alphabetically), and in the blank spaces provided, rank the top three in the order in which you think they best fit your relationship problem. Do not rank more than three conflicts. The purpose of this exercise is to begin to focus, and if selecting only three is difficult, even that work will be important. Identifying a hidden inner conflict is a challenging thing to do; if the conflict were easier to name, after all, it probably wouldn't have as strong a hold on you.

We'll do much more work later on identifying your master conflict, but for now, this exercise will help you absorb all of the information about conflicts introduced in this chapter and will give you some insights to begin helping you sort out the underlying dynamics behind the problems you've been having. In the next chapter, we'll take a closer look at how these conflicts tend to make their way into our lives, and this will also help you target the issues that are most significant for you. You should revisit the list of conflicts below, as well as your selection of conflicts and their ranking, at any point along the way that you think doing so would be helpful. But don't close yourself off to the possibility that another master conflict might turn out to be a better fit in the end.

I've included several other master conflicts, as well as the most common ones I previously presented. This broader list offers you a wider variety of conflicts to determine which fits better with your relationship issues.

MASTER CONFLICT LIST

1. **Acceptance vs. Rejection:** One side of you wants to be accepted and approved of. The other side of you questions your worthiness. ____

2. **Adequacy vs. Inadequacy:** One side of you feels that you're an adequate, competent person. The other side of you believes you are inadequate and incompetent. ____

3. **Closeness vs. Distance:** One side of you needs to be close to someone. The other side of you feels more comfortable connected from a distance. ____

4. **Commitment vs. Freedom:** One side of you desires the stability and security that a commitment can bring. The other side of you needs to be free of restraints. ____

5. **Conformity vs. Rebellion:** One side of you wants to be conservative and traditional. The other side of you is attracted to a more liberal lifestyle, free of the boundaries and restraints of a traditional one. ____

6. **Control vs. Chaos (Control vs. Out of Control):** One side of you prefers order and peace. The other side of you is attracted to drama and chaos. ____

7. **Getting Your Needs Met vs. Caretaking:** One side of you wants to meet your own needs and at times put yourself first. The other side of you needs to be selfless. ____

8. **Giving vs. Withholding:** One side of you has a desire to give to others. The other side of you withholds from them. ____

9. **Justice vs. Injustice:** One side of you has a strong desire to resist or protest unfairness and injustice. The other side of you helps create those conditions. ____

10. **Legitimacy vs. Illegitimacy:** One side of you feels authentic and valuable. The other side of you believes you are an imposter or fake. ____

11. **Person vs. Object:** One side of you desires to be treated as a respected human being. The other side of you believes you're unworthy of this treatment because you aren't perfect. ____

12. **Power vs. Passivity:** One side of you has a need for control and power. The other side of you desires to be free of responsibility. ____

13. **Resolution vs. Misery:** One side of you has a strong need to resolve your problems and be happy. The other side of you blocks resolution and remains in a state of misery. ____

14. **Satisfaction vs. Disappointment:** One side of you feels comfortable and satisfied. The other side of you is in a chronic state of disappointment or dissatisfaction. ____

15. **Security vs. Risk:** One side of you fears risk and is compelled to be cautious in life. The other side of you craves the excitement of risky behavior. ____

16. **Self vs. Loyalty:** One side of you has a strong need to choose your own path in life and follow your own dreams. The other side of you feels that you must remain loyal to your parents and not stray too far from their lot in life or what they may want from you. ____

17. **Specialness vs. Ordinariness:** One side of you has a need to feel special, to set yourself apart from others. The other side of you believes yourself to be ordinary or less than average. ____

18. **Success vs. Sabotage (Big vs. Small):** One side of you feels a strong need to be successful. The other side of you is compelled to sabotage this success. ____

19. **Trust vs. Distrust:** One side of you is trustworthy. The other side of you cannot be counted on and may have ethical issues. ___

20. **Other:** Add any master conflicts you can think of that fit you better or that help you understand your problem better. _____

3

THE ORIGIN OF YOUR
MASTER CONFLICT

As I pointed out in the stories of particular couples, master conflicts generally arise out of our family experiences. For this reason, the best way to start taking control of your conflict is to understand your past. Philosopher George Santayana famously wrote, "Those who can't remember the past are condemned to repeat it," and master conflicts are, in a very deep way, largely about repeating the past. Some psychologists say the reason we replicate our history is that we're simply more comfortable with the familiar. Contemplating whether or not to divorce, a client once said to me, "I think I'll just stick with the devil I know rather than the devil I don't. My parents stayed married for years even though they were miserable. I guess I'm more about commitment." Others in the field believe that we repeat our past because it's the only guide we have for how to react in the present—it's all we know. This is similar to the concept of role modeling, which says that we basically learn how to behave by copying the behavior of someone close to us, usually one or both parents. A woman I treated, for example, learned to run from arguments with her husband by watching her mother do the same in her marriage. Still other mental health experts claim that we keep going back to the same well because we're trying to work through unresolved issues from our childhoods. While this is closest to my conflict-theory model of working with couples, by now you probably realize that I think we're trying to avoid pain rather than work through anything. Nevertheless, the best way to begin to come to grips with how your own family history may be the basis of master conflict is to examine the three major ways in which we tend to be impacted by family sources of conflict.

THE THREE MAJOR SOURCES OF THE MASTER CONFLICT

The Role of the Player (Active Participant)

The more involved you were in the dynamics of your family of origin, the greater the influence these dynamics will have had on the development of your master conflict. I'm talking about something your parents *repeatedly did or said to you to directly involve you—to make you a player.* For example, they may have put you in the middle of their arguments and expected you to take sides. This could lead to a *justice vs. injustice* master conflict. I remember treating a woman who always sided with her mother. I mean, she *always* saw her mother as the victim and her father as the villain. It made sense that as an adult, she saw herself as a victim in an unfair world. She couldn't trust men. No one could convince her that she could be safe with them.

Another example: Maybe your parents gave you too much

adult responsibility at a young age. I once treated a fourteen-year-old boy who had the task of preparing his parents' income taxes. He came to a session with his parents wearing a navy blue suit, black wingtips, and black horn-rim glasses—he looked like a real CPA. This could lead to a *getting your needs met vs. caretaking* conflict—not to mention a life of *pleasure inhibition* (the person just can't have fun in life—life is taken far too seriously). Let's take a more detailed look at a player's role in her family dynamics.

I saw the pain on Lena's face. At thirty-nine, Lena still suffered the ill effects of having spent her childhood with a "very selfish mother." Lena needed to vent—to protest this injustice. In all of our sessions, she leaned forward in her chair as if she were about to lunge at me. But her real purpose was to emphasize her points—to make sure I understood the injustice she had suffered at the hands of her mother. For example, she told me that her mother gave her dog away without asking. Her father was there but never uttered a peep. And her mother would refuse to take her to her dance lessons if it conflicted with her beauty parlor appointments.

Lena had a feisty personality—not surprising since she also was the oldest child in her family. It was fitting that she was the one who protested her mom's behavior, while her younger siblings hid. Dad tried to calm Lena down, but he always catered to his wife. The result? Despite her noble efforts, Lena never won a fight, because she could never enlist the full support of her father, no matter how childish her mother's behavior. As the battle losses mounted, so did Lena's distaste for injustice. Eventually she developed into a one-woman vigilante—waiting to do battle with injustice in all areas of her life. She was a terrific mother who always treated her four children with thoughtfulness and kindness. But the *justice vs. injustice* master conflict she inherited caused her to be overly sensitive to her husband, Chuck, who tried hard to please Lena yet always ended up as the bad guy. Lena felt like the victim—especially with adults.

I liked and admired Lena. She could be a hero to those with problems; she was the type of person you'd want on your side, someone you could trust in battle. But she sometimes fought unnecessary fights that led her to suffer great stress.

Repetitious verbal messages from your family are also important in the development of your master conflict. Let's say your parents put too much pressure on you to succeed in school. The classic example: "I'd bring home all A's and one B, and my father would always get on me for the B." Or "I was told I'd never amount to much—I'd always be a bum." This kind of message may lead to the master conflicts *success vs. sabotage (big vs. small)* or *acceptance vs. rejection.* To see how, consider the case of Josh, a forty-one-year-old university professor I treated.

He was one of the nicest and most caring men I'd ever met, but he was suffering from an *acceptance vs. rejection* conflict. Josh had many admirable qualities. In fact, he was considered a true genius at the university he taught at. So why did he need me? Josh came to see me because he was upset about his weight. He claimed that he'd been overweight as long as he could remember and because of it, took a lot of abuse from childhood peers. As an adult he suffered a lack of respect from his professional colleagues.

Josh's weight problem also caused him marital difficulty. His wife, Hannah, an assertive thirty-seven-year-old, admitted that she was turned off sexually by Josh's weight. She said that Josh was always overweight, but during the past two years, he had gained (at least) another seventy-five pounds. "I'm not going to sleep with him until he loses twenty to thirty pounds," she said. Josh's reaction: "No amount of prestige in the world can make up for the pain this weight problem has caused me. I can live with the abuse from the past and some of the crap I still get from the guys in the faculty club, but I'll never forgive myself if Hannah leaves me because of it."

Though Josh tried hard to diet and exercise, nothing seemed to work—that is, until we began to focus more exclusively on his family history. It turned out that Josh's weight problem was an ever-present topic in his childhood home. His father, a very thin perfectionist, often criticized Josh for being overweight. Josh recalled, "I couldn't get away from my weight issue. It was bad enough that I was physically carrying it around with me and suffering in school, but my dad had to rip me. My mother wasn't as tough on me about it, but she agreed with my dad."

Josh was in a painful conflict. He wanted to be accepted by others, especially his wife and father. This is what drove him to therapy—if he lost weight he would increase his chances of being accepted. But he was also angry—angry enough at all those who didn't accept him to rebel by staying heavy. This, of course, ensured that he'd continue to be rejected. Josh was stuck, and it was beginning to take a toll on his health. His blood pressure and cholesterol were out of control.

Having been drawn into the family dynamics as a player is not the only way that family drama can leave us with a major conflict; we can develop a nice-sized conflict even if we take a more passive position. Read on to see how.

The Role of the Witness (Passive Participant)

The second way you may have developed your master conflict is by *witnessing* the relational dynamic between your parents *time and again* without interacting in the dynamic. For example, seeing one parent constantly criticizing the other could trigger a *justice vs. injustice* master conflict like Lena's.

√KEEP IN MIND: You can develop the "same" master conflict by being a player or a witness . . . or both.

Take a look at how the master conflict *resolution vs. misery* developed in a fifty-year-old newspaper editor named Les and his wife, Allison, forty-seven, an ultrasound technician.

As smart as they were, Les and Allison couldn't figure out what to do with their marriage—break up, or commit to each other. Both partners were involved in long-term extramarital affairs, and even though they were completely aware of their situation, neither could make a decision: End their affairs and try and make their marriage work, or end their marriage and move on with their lives. To complicate matters, both of their lovers were married and unable to decide what to do with their marriages. Everybody was "stuck"!

Although this was one of the most excruciatingly painful relationship dynamics I've ever seen, Les and Allison still couldn't free themselves. It was as if they were trapped in a giant spiderweb, and, sadly, this horrible situation went on for years. Even the couple's two children were exasperated and wanted their parents to split up. But the affairs carried on, and the marriage, if you could call it that, endured. How could a couple live like this? What could cause a couple to be trapped in such a terrible dynamic for such a long time?

Les and Allison both had parents who fought constantly but

never resolved anything. "They just screamed and yelled at each other until they got tired," Les said. "But they'd start up again in the next day or two—guaranteed." Allison understood the pattern. "Yeah, there was never any closure in my house either," she said. "Neither of my parents would ever give in." In other words, both Les and Allison's parents role-modeled a contagious inability to problem-solve. They showed Les and Allison how it was possible to live in suspended animation. And, although I don't have a lot of evidence to prove it, I'll bet that their respective lovers also suffered from the same master conflict. Remember, they couldn't decide what to do with their marriages either.

Here's one of my favorite examples of how witnessing can affect one's master conflict. Keep in mind that witnessing is similar to role modeling, but because there is almost always a powerful emotional component, it is much more internalized and more difficult to change than simple role modeling. Check out the elusive Derek and his *commitment vs. freedom* conflict.

Derek was a successful entrepreneur and self-made millionaire. Tall and charismatic, he was a favorite of the ladies, and it was easy to see why. Derek came to counseling without his girlfriend, Amanda; he was cheating on her and he wanted to discuss his situation privately. It turned out that Derek had a pattern of keeping two women—a girlfriend and a secret lover. As soon as the girlfriend would pressure him to marry, he would leave her for his lover. Derek repeated this cycle throughout most of his adult life and was about to do it again with Amanda. Why didn't he just break up with Amanda and continue his pattern? Well, Derek claimed that he knew he had a problem and wanted to become a father before he turned forty.

Derek was a tough client. He was evasive and tried to spend

most of his therapy discussing the pros and cons of staying with Amanda. But I insisted that he stop. "Your obsessing is a waste of time," I explained. "It hasn't cured you so far. Why don't you humor me and try something different—let's explore your family of origin and see if we can get at the real problem." Derek reluctantly agreed.

Because Derek was very bright, he rapidly figured out the connection between his trouble with commitment and his family of origin. Derek's father was a successful businessman; he was also a chronic philanderer. "He had women all over the place," Derek recalled. Hearing this, I began to refer to Derek's dad as the Old Spice Man. Remember the Old Spice cologne commercials, in which the sailor had a different woman in every port? Derek got a kick out of the comparison, even though he knew I was trying to make a point. Anyway, Derek's mother knew about her husband's indiscretions, but she couldn't do anything to stop them. "Mom tried to unload my old man, but he talked his way out of trouble time and again," he said. Though Derek was annoyed with his mother's powerlessness, he felt sorry for her. He also greatly admired his studlike father, believing that a "real man would never allow himself to be controlled by a woman."

Derek's *commitment vs. freedom* master conflict was fueled by an identity crisis: If he committed to a woman, he would lose his identity as a man. I can't say whether Derek solved his conflict, because he stopped treatment prematurely. I heard that he'd married Amanda. Before we go on, here's another reminder:

√KEEP IN MIND: Your parents may have had the same master conflict you do and the same amount of

difficulty managing it. I'm sure they couldn't help themselves. Still, if they were able to manage their conflict, you might not be reading this book.

The Role of the Family Trauma

A single trauma or onetime traumatic event in your family of origin can also foster a master conflict (whereas repeated events would fall under the *player* and *witness* categories). It has to be a whopper of an experience, but I've seen it happen. A severe, unforgettable beating by a parent or having a parent die in front of you are a couple of examples. My client Jake experienced a trauma that unquestionably contributed to his *control vs. chaos (control vs. out of control)* master conflict and later had a profound effect on his marriage.

Jake, forty-three, dragged his wife, Angela, thirty-eight, into marriage counseling because her disorganization was driving him nuts. "She's a mess, and when I come home from work, the house is a wreck, I never get my messages, and the kids are wild," Jake said. Meanwhile, Angela complained that Jake was obsessive and couldn't tolerate disorder of any kind. "We've got four kids," she said. "How can he expect organization?"

It was pretty clear that this couple had a conflict about control—Jake was too "controlling" and Angela was "out of control." Where did it come from? I learned that Jake had suffered a severe trauma as a young boy. His father went jogging one day while Jake sat on a bench reading a book. When his father returned and approached where Jake was sitting, he had a heart attack. Jake started screaming and tried to give mouth-to-mouth resuscitation, but by the time the medics arrived, his father was dead. Jake was only ten at the time.

I don't think you'll be surprised to learn that this single family trauma contributed to Jake's *control vs. chaos* conflict. After experiencing the loss of his father at such a young age, Jake needed control over everything and everyone he got close to, especially his family. Angela's disorganization raised Jake's anxiety level beyond his capacity to cope, causing him to feel out of control. He admitted thinking about divorce even when his kids' toys were strewn around the house. Okay, but why the attraction to chaos? Why would Jake marry someone like Angela instead of someone who shared his obsession for order? Because Jake needed to bring order to chaos; it was his way of getting a shot at saving his father.

Angela's *control vs. chaos* conflict came from a different place: she was a *player* in her family of origin. She was raised by a domineering mother who constantly intruded on her space. "My mom used to root through my stuff all the time—that's one thing I really hated," Angela said. "But she didn't give a damn what I thought—I had to run away from home to get her to stop doing it." While Angela loathed the structure her mother provided, she also became dependent on it—and that was what attracted her to Jake. She longed for Jake's structure, but then rebelled against it to create chaos. The bottom line: Both Jake and Angela needed control and chaos to complete them as individuals and as a couple.

√KEEP IN MIND: **Even though you and your partner have the same master conflict, each of you can get it from different sources.**

Let's look at a case that's slightly less extreme. Mallory, thirty-nine, a divorced woman who barely eked out a living as a waitress, came to see me because she was in a relationship with another musician, Bryant, whom she described as "temperamental" and unwilling to make a commitment. I thought he was abusive and had severe intimacy issues, but Mallory was obsessed with him. "I can't stop thinking about Bryant," she said, tearfully. "Why won't he just be with me? I give him whatever he wants."

I tried to help Mallory see Bryant's shortcomings, but nothing registered with her. She was in love! So, my question: Why was such a nice woman hell-bent on settling for less than she deserved? After all, Bryant demonstrated over and over again that he'd never meet her needs. The answer was eventually revealed in her family of origin.

Mallory was an infant when her father, a commercial pilot, never returned home from a routine flight. Years later, her aunt told her that his plane went down as a result of a malfunction. Mallory said that her mother couldn't handle the stress of the death and never spoke of it. Mallory felt abandoned and rejected.

The bottom line: Mallory suffered from an *acceptance vs. rejection* master conflict. She believed she was accepted by both her parents, but she still suffered the abandonment of her father. Even though he didn't mean to leave her, his death was a form of abandonment. On top of that, her stepfather rejected her. What was the fallout? Mallory was a confused young woman. She wasn't sure she was a "keeper," so she picked men who were conflicted about whether to accept or reject her—men like Bryant. Mallory was very attracted to this type of man.

BIRDS OF A FEATHER? SIBLINGS
AND THEIR MASTER CONFLICTS

One of the confusing things about the ways in which our family experiences influence us is how different the effects can be for different siblings. Not only will different people respond differently to any given set of circumstances, but family experiences can be quite different for each sibling. The conflict you've internalized and the amount of influence it exerts on your life hinge on several factors, such as your birth order, the role you played in your family, your relationship with your parents, and, perhaps most important, your perception of what life was like at the time. So, for example, the sibling who took the role of a *player* might have had a different experience growing up in the same family than did the sibling who took the role of a *witness*. What's more, each of these siblings may have even developed different master conflicts. Here's the story of Jamie and his brother Allen.

Jamie, forty-three, a law school professor, came alone to see me to discuss problems in his eleven-year marriage. Although Jamie said he preferred marital therapy, his wife's therapist claimed that she wasn't ready for such treatment—she was too angry at Jamie, and she also needed more time to gain some personal insight. Because Jamie insisted on blaming all of his problems on his mother, he needed some individual therapy to learn how to take some responsibility for himself. His perspective sounded quite skewed to me. I listened to his complaints about her and noticed how one-sided he was in support of his father. He said his mother was so sensitive to criticism that she couldn't even have a conversation without her blowing up on him. If he registered any complaint against her, she would freak out. When he was a little kid, he thought she was really scary. At this point, he was used to her reactions and would just get very angry. By contrast, his dad is very laid back. Nothing seems to bother him.

Despite Jamie's chilling condemnation of his mother, I detected some evidence that he sometimes *baited* her into a fight; he was, indeed, a *player*. For example, he told me that he once confided in her that he was thinking about leaving his wife for a colleague. He told her this knowing that she had conservative values. He also knew that she loved her daughter-in-law and that she was concerned about the mental health of her grandchildren if her son's marriage dissolved. When I first heard this, I told Jamie I thought he was "looking for a fight." He didn't believe me. He saw his mother as the fighter, and an unfair one at that. It took him a year of therapy to see that he was holding his mother far too responsible not only for his stormy relationship with her but also for all his marital problems. It took him even longer to accept that he married a woman like his mother (highly sensitive and extremely controlling) so that he could do battle with her, and to play out a *justice vs. injustice* master conflict.

As luck would have it, Jamie's elder brother, Allen, happened to be in town to visit his parents, and he agreed to come in for a few sessions to help his brother. Allen was distraught about Jamie's marital strife, and he was disturbed by the ongoing drama between Jamie and his mother.

Allen's visits paid off primarily because he lent a different perspective to the treatment. He saw their mother as extremely supportive and his father as distant. Like me, Allen also believed that Jamie baited his mother. "I love you, Jamie, but you're always starting fights with Mom . . . sometimes over nothing," he said. Because of his own unique experience and perspective, Allen didn't share his brother's view or master conflict. He had no interest in fighting injustice as Jamie did. In fact, Allen had his own problems: an unruly *closeness vs. distance* conflict that contributed to his poor relationship with his father. Fascinating, isn't it? Two siblings from the same family of origin, yet each had different experiences, different perspectives, and in the end, different master conflicts.

It's rare when I get the opportunity to treat the marriages of several siblings, but there's no better way to make my point that siblings who grew up in the same household can be affected differently and develop completely different master conflicts. Here's a brief glimpse into a family's lives.

Over a ten-year time period, I treated three siblings—two brothers and their sister—and their respective spouses for marital difficulty. All three siblings were employed in the family heating and air-conditioning business, which was run with an iron fist by their sixty-two-year-old mother, Joan. Joan's husband started the business in his youth but passed away of a heart attack at sixty. Because Joan was always involved in the business in some capacity, it was only natural that she take sole command after her husband died, and she did so with enthusiasm. Joan was determined to make a large business even bigger.

Although Joan delegated responsibility to her three children, she treated them differently and they responded in kind. For example, Joan constantly criticized her eldest son, Dustin, forty-two, and always seemed to find a reason to pass him over for promotions. Dustin was the *player* in the family. He routinely fought with Joan about the way she ran the business, and she in turn would put him down. Dustin freely admitted that he hated his mother and that he could never please her. He said she always made him feel like a failure. When I saw Dustin and his wife in marital therapy, he suffered from a *success vs. sabotage* master conflict. His wife had brought him into treatment because he kept sabotaging his position in the family company and yet he was too afraid to seek a higher-paying job elsewhere.

Dustin's siblings didn't have anything nice to say about their mother either, but they took different routes in dealing with her. Dustin's younger brother, Bart, thirty-nine, hid from his mother rather than take her on. He was a *witness*. When I saw Bart in marital therapy with his wife—about three years after I had seen Dustin—Bart was suffering from a *person vs. object* master conflict. He treated himself and his wife in the cold, purposeful way his mother had treated him. He was able to avoid a *success vs. failure* conflict because he was rewarded for his passivity with generous raises and regular promotions. His mother even promoted him to vice president—a move that further infuriated his older brother.

Kristen, thirty-six, the youngest sibling, was also a *witness*. But rather than hide from her mother, she kept her feelings to herself, ignored her own needs, and openly supported Joan. Unlike Bart, Kristen wasn't rewarded for her good behavior, because her mother felt that Kristen should marry and get her needs taken care of by a man, not by the company. When I saw Kristen in marital therapy—two years after I had seen Bart—she was in the throes of a *getting your needs met vs. caretaker* master conflict. Catering to an abusive, alcoholic husband for more than fifteen years, she finally exploded and dragged him into therapy after she caught him having sex with her best friend. Three siblings with three different master conflicts.

NEGATIVE EXPERIENCES IN ADULTHOOD
AND THE MASTER CONFLICT

A negative life event such as an affair is rarely the "cause" of serious relationship problems. The affair simply inflames a couple's master conflict and then all hell can break loose. This is the reason a couple might think that they were darn near perfect before their symptoms showed up . . . but they weren't. The truth is that their master conflict was only under control or manageable prior to the negative event. When the event occurred, it triggered the outbreak or "inflammation" of their master conflict, causing it to become unmanageable.

I saw proof of this while supervising a medical psychologist in a cancer unit of a large hospital. The psychologist was primarily responsible for treating couples where one or both partners were battling cancer; her role was to help them adjust to the stress of confronting a life-threatening illness. Going into this arena, I was sure I'd find that the disease created new conflicts for all of the suffering couples. But I was wrong; no new dynamics developed. What happened? Most of the master conflicts that were already in place got worse—a pattern I noticed time and again over a period of years.

So, a negative event or trauma in adulthood—be it an affair, a serious illness, or even a devastating change to one's financial situation—can make a master conflict less manageable and more destructive. If you've ever injured yourself and caused an inflammation of your soft tissue, you probably know how hard it is to get the inflammation down. Usually a few weeks of rest and a lot of anti-inflammatory medication are needed. Well, an inflamed master conflict can be just as, if not more, painful and damaging, but instead of causing pain to the body, an unruly master conflict causes relationship pain.

However, this isn't always the case. Sometimes a trauma can actually reduce the negative impact of an inflamed master conflict. To be more specific, it can increase mutual empathy and strengthen a couple's bond. For example, a minority of couples from the cancer unit did become closer. We also know that many couples have been able to improve their marriages following an affair, separation, death of a parent, even the death of a child. Still, these couples have their work cut out for them. Not only must they learn to cope with the negative behavioral trauma or event, they must also get the inflamed master conflict back under control. This is why it's best for couples to get into treatment as soon as they sense serious or chronic relationship difficulty—in other words, before the master conflict becomes inflamed enough to cause a trauma to the relationship.

Take the case of Oliver, thirty-nine, and his wife, Anne, thirty, a couple with a *giving vs. withholding* master conflict. Oliver left Anne because he felt she was unsympathetic when his best friend died of cancer at age forty. "Anne's not a warm person," he complained. "When my friend died she didn't seem to care. I knew the guy since second grade—we were inseparable. Hell, she didn't even want to go with me to the funeral. I was so upset, I started having panic attacks. I thought I was next. My lovely wife told me to get over it. She said I had better genes than my friend." Adding trauma to trauma, Oliver moved out of the family home and into a motel, but at least he still managed to come to the therapy sessions. Listen to one of their exchanges.

> **Anne:** I can't believe you left me because I didn't feel the same way you did about your friend's death. I do everything for

you. I put up with your lateness. I listen to your never-ending problems at work. And I never complain about your ridiculous spending habits, which, by the way, really irritate me. I can't be perfect. I'm definitely not Nancy Nurse.

Oliver: Like I don't do a lot for you! I put up with your limitations on our travel because of your bad back. And I deal with your constant jealousies of my sister. I also work really hard. I not only take care of you, I also take care of my mother. What do I ask for? Some sympathy! You showed more of it when our fish died. How do you think that makes me feel?

Anne: I care about you, but the truth is I never really liked your friend that much.

Oliver: *(Tearing up)* It's not about my friend. I think you just don't love me.

Anne: My God! I've never seen you cry. Am I really that important to you?

Both traumas—the death of Oliver's friend and his leaving Anne—initially strengthened the couple's master conflict. But in the end, these events actually reduced its power. Anne was very moved by Oliver's emotion and need for her. "I was shocked when he cried over me," she told me. "That was the first time he ever showed me his emotions. I had no idea I was causing him so much pain." After a few weeks of treatment, Anne softened, Oliver moved back into the house, and the couple continued to work on their *giving vs. withholding* master conflict.

LIFE CAN BE GOOD:
POSITIVE EXPERIENCES IN ADULTHOOD
AND THE MASTER CONFLICT

A positive life event can also affect a master conflict. Though it doesn't inflame it the way a negative experience can, it still throws it off balance by "choosing" one side of your conflict for you, usually before you are ready to make a choice. I liken it to being thrown into a pool and told to swim. Sure, it's scary as hell at first—even good change is painful—like ripping up old scar tissue. But if you can settle into your new situation, you'll probably end up feeling better than ever, because whether you were ready or not, you were forced to make strides toward controlling your master conflict.

As with a negative experience, a positive event can't resolve a master conflict, only make it more manageable. For example, if you're able to finally land that major promotion or buy the house you've always wanted with your own funds, your *success vs. sabotage* master conflict may improve. You may still experience some anxiety in the process of becoming more successful. After all, you'll be thrust into success while one side of you still wants to fail. But if you can get used to your success, you'll be that much more in control of your master conflict and no doubt happier.

Debbie, forty-four, and Sid, fifty-three, are perfect examples of this—a depressed couple whose master conflict became more manageable because of what they both called "a miraculous event." Sounds intriguing, doesn't it? Let's see what this couple was talking about.

When Sid and Debbie started therapy, they were fighting furiously about money. They had one daughter in college and another daughter about to go, while their son had just been accepted into medical school and needed financial assistance to cover the tuition. But Debbie was making only a modest salary as a receptionist at an insurance company. Sid, never good at coping with stress, had just quit his job as a low-level actuary because of the massive workload and a tyrannical boss.

Okay . . . Sid was stressed. But you might wonder why he wouldn't stick with his job at least until his family was in a better financial situation. Wouldn't quitting at such a crucial time cause him even more stress? Believe it or not, the couple didn't fight over this move. Sid desperately wanted to get away from his "micro-managing" boss. Debbie feared that Sid would have an early heart attack like his father, so she wanted him to leave as well. No, the real problem wasn't Sid's untimely decision to stop working. The culprit, as usual, was the couple's master conflict. This was made evident by the fact that both partners were highly educated—both had master's degrees—but were working in jobs and at salary levels that were beneath them, behavior indicative of a *success vs. sabotage* conflict. Both Debbie and Sid wanted more out of life, but . . .

While Sid picked up some part-time work at his brother's appliance store, Debbie, who'd become increasingly anxious, made a bigger move. She landed a higher-paying job as an executive secretary at a pharmaceutical company. But it wasn't enough. As the bills mounted and the looming educational costs closed in, the couple's *success vs. sabotage* master conflict became more and more unbalanced—they were leaning far too much in the direction of sabotage or failure than they could tolerate. The couple came to therapy when the conflict became not only emotionally and financially intolerable but physically troublesome as well. Both had difficulty sleeping, and Sid's stomach was more acid than a truck battery. Yes, things looked bleak. That is, of course, until fortune suddenly struck.

One evening, when Debbie and Sid arrived for their regularly scheduled visit, there was a different feel in the air. When I asked what was going on, Debbie said, "Oh nothing, except that my grandmother, whom I hadn't seen in years, died and left me millions." Sid followed with a wry smile. "Yeah, isn't it weird? I guess neither of us has to work anymore. Now the major stressor is how to take care of all this money. But I think we can live with that."

That's easier said than done, Sid. You can't just pacify a master conflict with a large chunk of change. Why not? Because the couple's sudden success unbalanced the couple's master conflict, shifting it too far toward the success end of the conflict. And while this shift was certainly a welcome opportunity for the couple, they needed time in treatment to get used to their success and get their master conflict under control. Not only did they have to learn how to cope with the anxiety of caring for the money, but they began to worry about losing it. Sid also expressed some guilt about no longer having to work. And this wasn't all this couple had to do. Even after they sorted out their financial issues, their master conflict was affecting other areas of their lives—areas in which they sabotaged personal success, such as the bedroom. For example, because of his performance anxiety, Sid had sexual difficulty. Instead of comforting and reducing Sid's anxiety, Debbie overreacted and increased his stress. Debbie and Sid's choice: to stop treatment after their windfall, or continue therapy and try to get a better grip on their master conflict. To their credit, they decided to stay in treatment and got their conflict even more under control.

THE RELATIONSHIP DEVELOPMENTAL LIFE CYCLE AND THE MASTER CONFLICT

Just as individuals go through a series of developmental life stages, so do couples. And just as significant *unexpected* external events can impact a master conflict, so can the *expectable* changes that accompany the relationship life cycle. We may not know exactly when these anxiety-provoking changes are coming or how we'll react to them, but we know they're headed our way sooner or later. They generally include those listed in the figure below.

Relationship Life Cycle Stages

Young Couple

Getting married/settling into a long-term partnership
Starting a career
Having children

Midlife Couple

Children leave home/empty nest experience
Questioning life choices
Male and female menopause

Senior Couple

Coping with declining health and old age
Death

At all phases of the life cycle, our master conflicts can be disturbed. Let's see how couples at each stage fared.

Young Couple

Brett and Heather, who were in their mid-twenties, suffered from a *commitment vs. freedom* master conflict. Although they'd been married only six months, they were already having difficulty deciding where to live—the reason they came to treatment. Heather wanted to remain in New Jersey, near her parents and grandparents; Brett preferred to relocate to the Pacific Northwest, where his former college roommates promised to install him in a lucrative position in their successful new company. Up to this point the couple's master conflict showed itself only in a couple of minor breakups when they were in college. By the time I saw them, it had cost them their short marriage. Neither would budge, so they decided to divorce in the first phase of their relationship cycle.

Midlife Couple

Henry and Wanda, both in their early fifties, had been married twenty-six years; their three daughters were twenty-three, twenty, and eighteen. The couple's *closeness vs. distance* conflict remained relatively dormant until their last child went off to college. Both Henry and Wanda missed their children, as most couples do, and now had no children at home to focus on. They discovered that all that time they'd been living in a "child-centered relationship." That is, they unconsciously used their daughters as buffers against marital closeness. When the last child left for college, Henry and Wanda were left in unfamiliar territory—and terrified of being close. The couple sought treatment because they were constantly fighting about everything and nothing. Every little thing that went wrong in their marriage provided the couple with fertile ground for an argument. In essence, the relationship was safe until they entered midlife and experienced the loss of their marriage buffer (the children).

Senior Couple

Fred and Mildred, a couple in their mid-sixties, had been married forty years. After retiring as the owner of an automobile dealership, Fred was diagnosed with lung cancer. Although the couple got along well before Fred's illness, when Fred required more attention and care than usual, the couple's *giving vs. withholding* conflict reared up, and they began to fight furiously. Mildred recalled all the times that she felt Fred had withheld his affection, money, and attention, and she decided that she didn't want to help him fight his cancer. Reacting to Mildred's emotional withdrawal, Fred got in touch with his long-held resentment for his wife, who had withheld sex from him. Considering their ages, financial situation, and the years invested in their marriage, the couple decided to stay together, even though their relationship remained far from loving and romantic. "We're like two friends now. We don't fight much anymore, but we're not very affectionate either. It's still better than going our own way at this age," Mildred said.

Specific psychological struggles are associated with different stages of the relationship life cycle, as are certain master conflicts. For example, conflicts around commitment, conformity, and loyalty tend to show up in younger couples; conflicts around adequacy, commitment, competence, and disappointment are often evident in midlife couples; and conflicts about adequacy, caretaking, competence, and giving frequently manifest themselves in senior couples. Considering the life stage of your relationship can be helpful to you in determining which master conflict may be responsible for your relationship problems.

YOUR PORTABLE MASTER CONFLICT

Once your master conflict is internalized or taken in, it becomes a part of you. It's portable; you can take it anywhere you go. During one couple's session, I remember hearing Ted tell his wife, Tara, "Instead of spending our money on therapy, let's move to Florida and get away from it all." What they didn't realize is that their master conflict could function very well in Florida, North Carolina, Mississippi, or any other part of the South or North or Midwest.

Joan and Phillip decided to travel rather than stay in treatment. And so they did—all over the world. But I heard from another client couple, friends of Joan and Phillip, that they fought in nearly every country they visited. Apparently, their master conflict also had a passport.

Miranda and Juan learned the hard way about their master conflict's multinational profile. A job transfer prompted the couple to move to Brazil, but they ended up needing long-distance telephone counseling sessions to cope with their *trust vs. distrust* master conflict. My first call from Miranda went roughly like this:

Miranda: *(Calling from Brazil)* Dr. Betchen, this is a beautiful country, and the people are wonderful. But even though I love it here, we're having more problems than we did in

Jersey. I think we need to start telephone sessions. Will you do that for us?

Dr. B.: *(Joking)* Sure. But see what happens when you leave Jersey!

Miranda: *(Laughs)* Actually, we didn't begin to have problems until after we settled down. At the beginning, we were getting used to the environment, so we didn't have time to get into our stuff. Now that we're organized, we're back at it. We really thought this change would bring us closer together, but we're still having trouble trusting each other.

I think you get my point: You can't run away from your master conflict, because it lives inside you. Remember the comedian David Brenner? A South Philadelphian, Brenner used to make fun of New Jersey. Who from Philly doesn't? Anyway, Brenner said that driving in Jersey isn't really that hard. The punch line: You just need to remember that Jersey has one tree—but it follows you everywhere you go. Well, your master conflict is your "one" tree.

Now it's time for you to assess the impact your own family history has had on you and on your master conflict. Completing the next two exercises will lead to a greater understanding of yourself and your family and will be invaluable in helping you pinpoint what your master conflict is and eventually coming to terms with it.

FAMILY OF ORIGIN IMPACT TEST

Put a check next to the statements that apply to you.

1. At least one of my parents repeatedly criticized/criticizes me. (2) ___

2. My feelings were/are never very important to my parents. (1) ___
3. My parents never admitted/admit they're wrong. (1) ___
4. One parent was/is easier to talk to than the other. (1) ___
5. One parent or both parents told/tell me their problems. (2) ___
6. One or both parents had/have the same problem I have. (3) ___
7. One or more of my siblings had/has the same problem I have. (2) ___
8. The problem is just as painful today, if not more painful than it was in the past. (3) ___
9. My parents succeeded/succeed in getting me to take sides in their arguments. (3) ___
10. My parents never seemed/seem to resolve their arguments. (1) ___
11. I've always felt sorry for one parent. (1) ___
12. I am/was the "favorite" child of one or both parents. (1) ___
13. I am the eldest child in my family. (2) ___
14. I am the youngest child in my family. (1) ___
15. I am an only child. (3) ___
16. One parent always seemed/seems to be in control or to get their way. (1) ___
17. One parent was/is more responsible than the other. (1) ___
18. One parent seemed/seems more dependent on the other. (1) ___

19. One parent was/is more loyal than the other. (1) ___
20. I had problems getting along with my siblings as a child. (1) ___
21. My family moved a lot when I was a child. (1) ___
22. My partner and I interact the way my parents did. (4) ___
23. My partner and I interact the way his/her parents did. (4) ___
24. My partner reminds me of my least favorite parent. (4) ___
25. My partner criticizes me repeatedly about the same problem. (3)
    ___

    Score: ___

Now add up the points in the parentheses next to each statement you checked and record the total score in the space provided at the bottom of the list. If you scored 15 or more points, your master conflict was influenced by your family of origin.

FAMILY OF ORIGIN TRAUMA LIST

Check off any of the traumas you've experienced in your family of origin to determine their impact on your master conflict.

1. My parents divorced when I was a child. ___
2. I rarely or never saw one of my parents when growing up. ___
3. One or both of my parents died when I was a child. ___
4. One or more of my siblings has hurt me deeply. ___
5. The parent I was closest to died when I was an adult. ___
6. Someone in my family had a serious illness when I was a child.
   ___
7. I had a serious illness when I was a child. ___
8. I was abused or neglected as a child. ___

9. One parent had a substance abuse problem. ___
10. Both parents had substance abuse problems. ___

If you checked at least one of these traumas, your family of origin probably has had at least a moderate impact on your conflict and on your current relationship.

Now complete the next two exercises to determine to what degree external life events (experiences outside your family of origin) have had an impact on your master conflict.

EXTERNAL LIFE EVENT IMPACT TEST

Read the following statements and put a check next to the events you've experienced.

1. I've experienced a positive, life-changing event in my lifetime. (1)
   ___
2. Now I know my dreams will probably never come true. (4) ___
3. My financial situation has changed for the better. (1) ___
4. I'm more religious or spiritual than I used to be. (1) ___
5. A negative experience or event has helped to improve my life. (2)
   ___
6. A negative experience or event has made my life worse. (4) ___
7. A former significant partner has hurt me deeply. (2) ___
8. I'm mistreated at work. (1) ___
9. I won or earned more money than I ever believed I would. (1) ___
10. I've failed at reaching one or more of my major goals in life. (5) ___
    Score: ___

If you scored 8 or more points, your life experiences outside your family of origin have affected your master conflict in some way.

Check off one or more of the traumas you've experienced in your life outside your family of origin to determine whether they have had an impact on your master conflict.

EXTERNAL LIFE TRAUMA LIST

1. I experienced a debilitating or life-threatening illness as an adult. ___

2. My partner has a serious or life-threatening illness. ___
3. My partner was seriously ill during our relationship. ___
4. I'm physically disabled. ___
5. I was physically disabled for six months or longer. ___
6. My partner is physically disabled. ___
7. My partner was physically disabled for six months or longer. ___
8. I was sexually assaulted as an adult. ___
9. I was physically assaulted as an adult. ___
10. I have a substance abuse problem. ___
11. My partner has a substance abuse problem. ___
12. My partner has had an affair. ___
13. My partner is having an affair. ___
14. My partner left me in the past. ___
15. One of my children has a substance abuse problem. ___
16. One of my children is seriously ill or disabled. ___
17. One of my children was seriously ill or disabled. ___
18. One of my children has died. ___
19. My best friend has died. ___

20. I was fired from a job I love. ___

21. I was fired from a job that I desperately needed. ___

22. I've been unable to get a job for more than six months. ___

If you've checked off even one trauma, trust me, life has had an impact on you and your master conflict.

4

THE DEFENSES WE USE

Why are our master conflicts so tenacious? Why don't we resolve them more naturally as we age? Well, one key reason is that there are powerful mechanisms in our brains that can prevent us from confronting our conflicts head-on. The philosopher Friedrich Nietzsche wrote: "Where my honesty ceases, I am blind and I also know I want to be blind." If we don't want to see something—usually because it's just too painful or too anxiety-provoking to deal with—we have a retinue of defense mechanisms that allow us to blind ourselves. These unconscious defenses play a powerful role in helping us deny and distort reality just enough to avoid challenging our conflicts and the unbearable decision of choosing one side over the other. Of course, sometimes it's good to forget about a terrible incident; after all, you do need to move on with your life. But protecting a master conflict that has begun to cause serious problems in your relationship will only make you and your partner more and more unhappy.

In this chapter I will introduce the four defenses that I see most often in treating couples with master conflicts, in the hope that doing so will help you see how you might be engaging in one or another of them, and thus become more prepared to commit to staring your master conflict down. These four mechanisms are denial, rationalization, projection, and repression. We may use more than one of these defenses at the same time, but we all have our favorites. I'm sure that they are familiar to you, but what may not be clear is how they've been playing a role in perpetuating your inner conflicts.

Denial is the refusal to acknowledge or accept unpleasant reality—you act as if a painful event, thought, or feeling doesn't exist. Using denial helps you hide the flaws of a potential partner. In other words, your conflict can use denial to ignore any "red flags" that would warn you of danger, even though they may be glaringly obvious to your friends and family. I had a woman in therapy named Trish, a forty-eight-year-old divorcee. Trish strongly believed that Patrick, fifty, was the next man of her dreams.

Dr. B.: I'm not as sure about this guy as you are.

Trish: Why not?

Dr. B.: Don't you have any questions about him?

Trish: Not really. I've gone out with him only three times, and it's been wonderful.

Dr. B.: How do you feel about having to pay for all the dates?

Trish: No problem. His credit cards were revoked but he'll get them back soon.

Dr. B.: Trish, that doesn't usually happen for no reason. To boot, he doesn't even seem embarrassed by the fact that you have to pay.

Trish: *(Angry)* I think he's a responsible guy. If it were up to you, I'd never remarry. You see problems in every person I go out with.

Trish was so upset with me that I didn't think our therapeutic relationship would survive—and it didn't. Ironically, Trish stopped therapy soon after she learned I was right about Patrick. I never met Patrick, but I can tell you that Trish left me in order to preserve her master conflict of *satisfaction vs. disappointment.* She had an extensive history of impulsively falling hard for men—that is, being immediately satisfied—only to become extremely disappointed with them. And she played the same dynamic with me. At the beginning of treatment, she couldn't get enough therapy. She scheduled multiple sessions in advance and, I believe, greatly exaggerated my value to her. But in the end, you can see that even though I was trying to spare her future pain, she found a way to become disappointed with me. I did my best not to let her down, but it wasn't good enough. As friends and family members may discover when they try to point out to a loved one that he or she is stuck in a conflict, our denial can be truly vehement. So it does its trick not only by helping us to delude ourselves but also by warding off the people in our lives who might help us recognize that we are suffering because of a conflict.

Rationalization can help you create logical but false excuses to justify unacceptable behavior. On many occasions, I've seen people minimize or downplay their partners' problems. Consider this exchange from a session I had with Valerie, a thirty-six-year-old accountant, and her husband, Greg, a forty-two-year-old lawyer. Val was very angry with Greg, because she believed he was always staring at other women.

> **Dr. B.:** Val, did you notice that Greg stared at other women before you married him?
> **Valerie:** Yeah. He's done this as long as I've known him. Once

we went to Myrtle Beach together, and it was awful. He couldn't take his eyes off the women, especially the ones in bikinis. You have to understand, Greg doesn't just take a quick glance—I could handle that—he stares so hard, he turns his whole body around as they walk by. It's humiliating to me.

Dr. B.: So, Val, if Greg did this kind of thing before marriage, why did you marry him?

Valerie: Back then, I believed that his behavior was normal for a guy his age. I thought that once we were married and I had more sex with him, he wouldn't feel the need to ogle.

Valerie and Greg shared the *acceptance vs. rejection* master conflict. Unconsciously, each found a way to be accepted and rejected (or disapproved of) at the same time. They accepted each other in marriage, but Val felt humiliated and rejected by Greg's ogling behavior. In order to marry Greg and maintain her master conflict, Val had rationalized that Greg's behavior was "normal for a guy his age." She also rationalized that he stared at other women because she hadn't been giving him enough sex—something she felt she could easily fix.

Projection is a perfect defense for couples—ideal for maintaining a master conflict. Why? Because when you project, you basically blame your partner for having certain thoughts and feelings about you that, in reality, you have about them. It's as if you're a movie projector, shining your internal movie onto their blank screen. Projection is incredibly valuable to couples because it allows each partner in the relationship to avoid being the "bad guy." For example, if you're angry with your mate, but you feel uncomfortable with anger or confrontation, you can project your anger onto him or her. This way, you can convince yourself that he or she is mad at *you*—you're the victim and your mate is the persecutor. Partners are able to collude in maintaining their shared master conflict as long as one partner projects and the other accepts the projection. A healthy mate will not only avoid projecting onto his or her partner but also reject any oncoming projections from that partner.

Here's an example of a man who was projecting in order to avoid dealing with his *commitment vs. freedom* master conflict. For her part, his wife unconsciously supports his projection by buying in to his projection onto her.

> **Reese:** You're always mad at me for something. You sound angry whenever you speak to me.
> **Amy:** Really? I didn't think I was so angry, but maybe I am.
> **Dr. B.:** Reese, I haven't heard any anger coming from Amy. The anger I hear usually comes from you.
> **Reese:** I don't feel angry, just frustrated.
> **Amy:** I may be guilty—I'm not so sure. Sometimes I don't know when I'm pissed about something.

Reese kept projecting his anger onto a cooperative Amy despite my attempts to make him "own" his projection. So, how to break this logjam? My first step was to ask Reese if he would see me by himself for a session or two. He did, and it turned out that he was a monster projector. Reese revealed to me that he had fallen in love with another woman and wanted to leave Amy. He said he was "crazy" about this other woman and wanted badly to be with her, yet felt too guilty to divorce. "I don't know if I could live with myself if I left Amy and the kids," Reese explained. "I'd always think of myself as a bad husband and father. My best friend left his wife and children twenty-five years ago, and he tells me he's never recovered from it." Reese was manufacturing anger and frustration for Amy because he was stuck in a commitment conflict that he couldn't resolve. Amy, meanwhile, was too conflicted to reject his projections. In the example below, see if you can determine which mate was projecting, as well as what master conflict was being protected.

> **Larry:** I'd love to look for a new car this week. You know mine is always breaking down. What do you think?
>
> **Fern:** No problem. I'd like to get one also . . . maybe a Maserati. Do y-o-o-o-u mind?
>
> **Larry:** Sorry. I was just asking.
>
> **Fern:** I'm just tired of you putting all your needs first. What about my needs?
>
> **Larry:** I guess I can be sort of selfish. I don't mean to be.

If you determined that Fern was projecting onto a very cooperative Larry, you're right. It turns out that she was in the grip of a *getting your needs met vs. caretaking* conflict and she projected her anger and frustration with herself onto Larry, who accepted her projections with guilt.

Repression helps you bury undesirable thoughts and feelings from consciousness. It can be especially effective in warding off the horrors associated with previous trauma. Repression is considered the "mother" of all defense mechanisms, because all defenses consist of a certain amount of repression. Repression is *key* to master conflict theory. You must bury your past—and at least half of your conflict—in order to maintain it. Although repression is everywhere, I see it most when I'm trying to help a couple look into their past. It's amazing how people can simply forget what a parent, former mate, or present partner has done to them or how they've been affected by these significant players. You will see the impact of repression and how it relates to Harry and Jesse's master conflict of *justice vs. injustice.*

Dr. B.: Harry, are your parents still alive?

Harry: No, my mother died a few years ago, and my dad died more than twenty years ago.

Dr. B.: And you're in your late thirties. So that means you were a teenager when he died.

Harry: Yeah.

Dr. B.: Do you miss him?

Harry: Not anymore. I don't think about him much. My mother remarried, so I think of my stepfather as my dad.

Dr. B.: Jesse, are your parents still alive?

Jesse: Wait! Harry, don't you think you ought to tell the doctor what happened to your dad?

Harry: What do you mean?

Jesse: I mean the way he died.

Harry: Is that important?

Dr. B.: Let's see.

Harry: Well, I came home one night and found him hanging in the basement. He'd tied a rope to a ceiling shaft and hung himself.

Dr. B.: Was he actually dead when you found him?

Harry: I forgot about this, but he died in my arms. He was still alive when I cut him down. I tried to give him mouth-to-mouth resuscitation, but it didn't work. He was gone by the time the rescue squad got there.

Dr. B.: Did he have any last words?

Harry: No.

Dr. B.: I'm sorry, Harry. That sounds awful.

Harry: Yeah, I think at first I was in shock, but soon I just pushed it out of my mind.

Dr. B.: Does it ever pop out?

Harry: Rarely, though it can a little bit if I see a father-son movie. I get angry and feel ripped off.

Harry didn't think his father's death had an impact on his master conflict, but Jesse admitted that Harry acts "cheated," and to make up for it, he tends to be overly demanding as a husband. In choosing Harry, Jesse unconsciously set herself up to be treated unfairly. But, to do her part to support their mutual conflict, Jesse often underworked.

You also can repress what may seem to be a very minor negative incident or experience for the sake of matching up your master conflict with someone else's. Why? Because repression isn't limited to trauma. Tina and Cameron are a great example. Let's see how Tina's repression of one seemingly small incident, if she had recognized it, could have given her an indication of what awaited her once she married Cameron.

A professional couple in their mid-twenties, Tina and Cameron came to see me even though Tina had made up her mind to divorce; she promised Cameron she'd attend one session as a "going-away present." During the session, Tina talked about how mistreated and unappreciated she felt in her brief marriage. Cameron didn't deny his cold behavior, but he wasn't very apologetic. In fact, when he realized his efforts to change Tina's mind about the marriage were futile, he stormed out of the session before the hour was up.

Fearing her relationship radar was off, I convinced a very skeptical Tina to stay for a few sessions. Given her youth, I knew the odds were strong that she would remarry, and I wanted to help her avoid another disaster. I wanted her to figure out why she chose Cameron in the first place. But when I asked her to take a hard, cold look at her reasons, she stuck with her defense that Cameron was simply a "great actor" and that during their dating courtship, there were no clues to suggest that he would be so cold and cruel once they were married.

I kept trying to find a way to get her to see the truth, so I began by investigating their premarital relationship more closely. After I encouraged Tina to tell me anything about Cameron that had rubbed her the wrong way early on—even if she didn't think it was that important—she finally told me this:

Tina: Cameron and I went to the same college. One winter night, I stayed up until midnight to type one of his papers even though I had finals the next day. I walked to his dorm in the snow and surprised him. But, instead of being happy with me, he took the paper out of my hands, put it on the table, and told me to go back to my room because it was late.

Dr. B.: That's it? He didn't even say "Thanks"?

Tina: No. I know there was another incident like this about a year or so later, but I don't remember any details. Anyway, I still don't think it's such a big deal. I quickly forgot about the whole thing until you made me think of it.

Dr. B.: So, at the time, you didn't think that experience was giving you a glimpse into your future with Cameron?

Tina: Not really. It was only a paper.

Cameron's reaction to Tina that cold snowy night many moons ago should have been a warning to Tina of what was to follow, but she repressed it, and she continued to deny the message it should have sent her even after the memory had resurfaced. This is a good example of how defense mechanisms can work in league with one another.

A THERAPIST'S TALE

The many ways in which our defense mechanisms kick in when it comes to supporting our maintenance of our master conflict are amazing. An example from my own life involves the use of denial to justify irrational behavior that was in service to the master conflict that my wife and I share. That's right. I'm not immune to the pull of master conflicts. When I was a twenty-one-year-old college senior, a friend set me up on a date with a nineteen-year-old junior who'd expressed an interest in me. I barely knew her, but she was a psychology major like me; I'd spoken to her only once, about the psychology club. But when we finally met for dinner, I quickly noticed that I was very attracted to her. The next thing I knew, we were engaged. Bam! What happened?

Well, I was aware that my future wife had several attributes that attracted me. I knew I had a special place in my heart for Italian girls. I was of the opinion that most of them possess a combination of commitment and passion for their relationships—key ingredients for the mating life. What ultimately sealed the deal with her, though I didn't realize it at the time, was the fact that we shared a similar conflict: we both were ambivalent about our stations in life. We wanted to be successful but feared rising too high—a conflict born of having grown up with both loyalty and distaste for our parents' respective values and the neighborhoods where we were raised. We shared the *self vs. loyalty* conflict. To quote Renée Zellweger's character in the movie *Jerry Maguire,* this conflict "had me at hello," and it has been a major factor in our marriage as we consistently try to strike a balance between each other's successes and failures. For example, if I act ambitious or come up with an idea that may make us more money or elevate our socioeconomic status, my wife will unconsciously find a way to shoot me down. She often refers to me as a "foolish dreamer." But if I don't earn enough income, she will needle me about it until I figure out a way to make some extra dollars. If she isn't showing any creative ambition, I will pester her about her lack of drive. Yet if she works too hard at her job, even if she is about to be promoted or get a substantial salary increase, I might encourage her to take off a week and relax with me. Our conflict is helpful at times, because it can keep us both in check. But without insight and management, it can certainly stir up problems for us. This reminds me of the Volvo incident, as we've come to call it.

It was 1993, and our second child had just turned two, when I decided to buy my wife a Volvo. I thought I'd feel better knowing that she and the kids were in a safe car, rather than the old jalopy she'd been driving. At the time, we were living very frugally in a town house, but I had secured my first decent-paying job, so money wasn't a huge issue. Plus, the finance charges were reasonable. My wife thought I was joking, but she packed up the kids and off to a Volvo dealer we went. While the three of them were playing around in the showroom, I looked at the cars and then called my wife over to meet the salesman and to choose a color for her beautiful new Volvo 940 Turbo, complete with moonroof and heaters in the seats. Well, my wife joined us all right, but she immediately started hyperventilating until the salesman, in a panic, found her a paper bag she could breathe into. She scared the heck out of everyone at the car dealership, especially me.

After buying the car, I told her that the incident at the dealership was connected to our *self vs. loyalty* conflict. Of course, she just rolled her eyes and told me I was crazy. "It happened because I'm out of shape and I was running around the showroom with the kids," she said. "If we had a stationary bike at home instead of that stupid treadmill machine, which I keep falling off, this probably wouldn't have happened."

About a month later, I went to the ATM machine to draw out $10 for lunch, only to find that my account was overdrawn by $9,000. I thought this couldn't be true, because I never kept that kind of money in my checking account. After some investigation, a bank representative told me that someone had made a check out to Volvo North America for $9,000 and, in the process, had overdrawn the account and bounced twenty-five checks meant for other expenses. Immediately, I suspected that my wife's conflict might be behind this mystery. I called her from the bank. Sure enough, my wife, usually a very careful woman, unconsciously (with the help of *denial*) paid off her new Volvo with funds we didn't have. Why?

When we talked it over, she and I agreed that while she loved the car, it also made her feel alienated from her parents and her old way of life. "Sometimes it's just too hard to leave the old neighborhood," she said, sighing. Basically, my wife's master conflict was so intolerable that she couldn't bear to make the car payments. Her solution? Drive the car, but pay it off as soon as possible, so that she wouldn't have to face the fact that she'd bought it—a reminder that she was now the proud, upper-middle-class owner of a brand new Volvo . . . and the Benedict Arnold of her family. (I have since gotten control over my conflict and now drive a Volvo. She drives a Subaru, and she no longer hyperventilates.)

THE PAST IS TOO EASY TO REPEAT

Another way in which our defense mechanisms can perpetuate the pain we may be enduring because of a master conflict is by preventing us from grappling with the real reasons that prior relationships didn't work. When we choose our first serious partner or our spouse, we often have no idea what role our master conflict played in the choice.

If that relationship ends and we still don't understand the role of our master conflict by the time we choose a mate for the second or third time, we tend to focus on the one thing we think ruined us the first time around—a dangerously narrow view. "I'll never marry an alcoholic again" is a good example. With the help of our defense mechanisms, we can make poor decisions a second, third, or—God forbid—fourth time around.

Of course, you might also consistently select healthy partners. If your beloved mate dies, for example, you may then gravitate toward another wonderful person. But I can't tell you how many times I've run into former clients who've ended treatment prematurely, "divorced," and remarried someone just like their former partners. And then there are the cases in which it *seems* that they've married someone different—for example, someone who is not an alcoholic—only to find out that there is an underlying similarity.

The person who managed not to marry an alcoholic might, for example, become involved with a different type of addict.

This is another reason why it's so important in analyzing your current relationship problems to grapple with whether or not a master conflict is at play. Otherwise you are that much more liable to opt to end the relationship and then get right back into another one, in which you'll eventually have very similar problems.

Take a look at Jon, a forty-one-year-old golf pro, who underestimated the power of his master conflict. He actually thought that his new female interest was the complete opposite of his wife, Mary, a forty-three-year-old pharmaceutical sales representative. Here's his story.

When we first met, Jon seemed to me a contradiction. His athletic physique belied his thoughtful, introverted, and somewhat passive personality. In a soft, barely audible voice, he began telling me how unhappy he was in his marriage to Mary, who seemed to prefer action to introspection. "At first I found Mary very exciting, but after a while, I began to see her as unloving," Jon said. "She seems more interested in her career and her extracurricular activities than our relationship."

Angry and hurt, Jon responded by having an emotional affair with a female golf pro he viewed as very caring and sensitive—seemingly the opposite of his brash, extroverted wife. After some discussion in therapy, however, Jon was shocked to discover that his new friend had the same master conflict that he and his wife shared: all were conflicted about resolving problems and making their lives better. I call this conflict *resolution vs. misery.* Jon, his wife, and his friend were all unhappy, yet they all had trouble committing to finding a solution to their unhappiness. Mary knew about Jon's relationship, but instead of trying to put an end to it, she busied herself with one activity after another. She even tried to avoid therapy—she looked for any excuse she could to miss the couples' joint sessions. Jon's friend was in a terrible relationship with a man she lived with for many years, yet she refused to seek treatment.

The inability or refusal to problem-solve was also a major factor in all three of the players or active participants' families of origin. All had lived under intolerable conditions as children while their parents did little to improve matters. Mary, Jon, and Jon's friend all had at least one abusive parent. "My mother and father-in-law were alcoholics. They were pretty mean people," said Jon.

Our defenses cause us to miss countless small cues that might otherwise alert us to the fact that we are deeply conflicted. And even when we do start to see the problem clearly, our defenses may lead us to minimize how serious the conflict is and to convince ourselves that the friction it's causing in the relationship will just go away eventually. You may well feel the forces of these defense mechanisms working on your mind as you continue with the project of analyzing your own master conflict. Be very wary of them. If you really want to come to a better resolution of your conflict and save your relationship, you will have to fight these powerful mechanisms, and the best way of doing so is to keep them present in your consciousness. Remind yourself about them regularly as you continue with the evaluation of your relationship through the course of this book; otherwise they may get the better of you and prevent you from coming up with a clear understanding of the conflict that you and your partner need to become aware of and do hard work on.

5

THE BIG THREE:
SEX, MONEY, IN-LAWS
AND
YOUR MASTER CONFLICT

Most of the couples I treat firmly believe that their problems stem from one of these "big three" issues. These are, in fact, the three most common issues that couples fight about. What I have generally found, however, is that the specific problems they are having in regard to these three issues are very often symptoms of a master conflict, not the cause of their problems. So in this chapter I will probe into two key questions:

1. *Why do these specific issues cause couples the most difficulty?*
2. *How are they connected to master conflicts?*

TROUBLE IN THE BEDROOM:
YOUR MASTER CONFLICT AND SEX

Why is sex a predominant issue in the lives of couples? The answer may seem glaringly obvious, but there are some deeper reasons that we should consider. First, sex is tied to our feelings of adequacy; nobody likes to feel sexually inadequate. Sex is also linked to our need to feel attractive to others—to be accepted and desired. We all want to be desired; it's a tremendous feeling when a partner can't keep his or her hands off of you. And, of course, whereas compliments about our sexual attractiveness and sexual prowess can be emotionally uplifting, criticism and rejection can be devastating. Whenever I treat a couple with a sexual issue, the partner without the sexual symptom feels rejected. Even if the symptom bearer suffers from a physical problem, it can be downright hard to convince the other partner not to take the mate's sexual problem personally.

I once saw a twenty-eight-year-old woman whose husband showed little interest in her. As it turned out, he had very low testosterone. She left him anyway because she was convinced that he was having an affair, hence, his lack of desire in their bedroom. Angry and hurt, she didn't even stick around long enough to give her husband's hormonal treatment time to take effect. "If it doesn't come naturally, it means it was not meant to be," she said, rather naively. A fifty-seven-year-old man in my practice still felt the effects of being told he had a small penis by a high-school girlfriend whom he saw as his dream girl. He blamed this message for his persistent erection problems in his marriage.

For all of these reasons, the nature of a couple's sex life is, indeed, the most accurate barometer of a couple's welfare. As sex therapist Barry McCarthy wrote, "When sexuality functions well in a marriage, it is 15 to 20% of the relationship, creating special feelings and energizing the bond. When sexuality is dysfunctional or nonexistent, it plays an inordinately powerful role, 50 to 75%, draining the marriage of intimacy and vitality."* My major point is that by applying the insights about master conflicts that I've introduced, you may well discover that the sex issues you are having stem from an underlying master conflict, and that the conflict may be the key reason that you have not been able to resolve your sexual issues as a couple. For example, if you suffer from an *acceptance vs. rejection* conflict, consider how that might lead both of you to have ambivalence about a healthy sexual relationship. If a part of your brain is insisting on your feeling rejected on a regular basis, then a thriving sex life may be a problem for you. You can readily see how this would also be true for the *adequacy vs. inadequacy* conflict. One side of you will be fighting against the feelings of adequacy that a healthy sex life almost surely brings with it.

With the *closeness vs. distance* conflict the connection is particularly clear to see. A good sexual relationship by its very nature makes two people feel very tightly bonded, and that would be a red flag for people who are conflicted about how much intimacy they want with a partner.

Take some time to think about how each of these other master conflicts would tend to throw a wrench into a couple's sex life:

---

* B. McCarthy, Relapse Strategies and Techniques with Erectile Dysfunction, *Journal of Sex & Marital Therapy* 25, 297–303.

Commitment vs. freedom
Conformity vs. rebellion
Control vs. passivity
Giving vs. withholding
Person vs. object

To see in more detail how the causal relationship can go from a master conflict to the sex life conflict, consider the story of one couple I counseled whose sexual problem was threatening their marriage. The issue came up because the wife was upset by her husband's low desire. But as we probed into their relationship further and further, it became clear to me that the couple's problems in their sex life stemmed from the *giving vs. withholding* master conflict.

Jim and Cara were a married couple in their mid-forties. Cara entered my office first and sat down in my leather love seat. Jim slowly followed but parked himself in a chair on the other side of the room. Jim was a teacher at a prep school. His body language and the expression on his face sent the message that he would rather have been anywhere else in the world than a marriage counselor's office.

A housewife, Cara held an associate's degree and wore a tube top and a thigh-skimming skirt with high heels. On her face there was a look of urgency; her eyes watered as if she was about to cry. "I can't believe I had to drag Jim here," she said, gently stroking her hair. "I don't understand how he can live like this; we haven't had sex in two years. I'm ready to give up. Do you think he's gay?" Jim smirked, then faced Cara and said in an angry tone, "That's ridiculous! I won't have sex with you because I don't like the way you dress. I've told you this a thousand times, but you don't believe me.

114

You look like an adolescent hooker. It's embarrassing! You always want everything your way! Even when we did have sex, it always had to be how, when, and where you wanted it. You've worn me out. You win. I'm just not that interested in having sex with you anymore."

Wiping a tear from her eye, Cara angrily responded, "Don't you dare blame our sexual problems on me! You were never really into having it from the beginning—your drive was always low. And another thing, can I help it if you have no taste and buy all your clothes from an L.L. Bean catalog? I've always dressed like this, and you know it. Besides, before we were married, you couldn't wait to show me off to your colleagues." Jim nodded in agreement. "That was then, and this is now," he said. "I think a teacher's wife should look respectable. Before, my colleagues were jealous, but now that you're my wife, they snicker behind my back. You just can't give in on anything, can you?"

While Jim and Cara couldn't have appeared any more different on the surface, it became clear, through their work in counseling, that they were bonded by a very powerful underlying *giving vs. withholding* master conflict. Jim gave Cara a lavish lifestyle, courtesy of a large inherited trust fund, but demanded that she live without physical and emotional love. He was actually insulted that she desired more than he already provided; he wanted her to accept the limitations of their marriage without complaint. So, part of Jim *gave* and part of him *withheld*.

Cara eventually admitted that she "at times" withheld her approval of Jim unless he conformed to her specific ways. A great example of this took place on the couple's vacation on the Costa del Sol. After several months of therapy, Jim finally got a little frisky and popped a Cialis to help him have sex with Cara. "I wanted to *ensure* a successful experience, so I used the medication as a backup," he said. You'd have thought this would please Cara, but upon seeing Jim's erection, she shook her finger at him and scolded, "Oh no . . . you used that medication, didn't you? Forget it. If you don't want me naturally, you can't have me at all."

Where did Jim's conflict come from? Jim's mother catered to his every need, but his father, an angry man, withheld love and nurturing. Jim described his dad as "very critical" and "hard to please." Because his mother had instilled the caretaking gene in Jim, he was able to give Cara all the material goods she desired. He expressed great pride in providing her with a big home, expensive cars, and extravagant family vacations. But because of his father's influence, Jim also insisted that Cara live without physical and emotional intimacy.

How about the origin of Cara's conflict? By treating her as his "special child," Cara's father taught her how to give, so she willingly gave Jim plenty of sex. But because her mother rejected and severely ridiculed her, she withheld her approval of him unless he conformed to her standards. Cara admitted that she refused to change her style of dress because it turned men's heads, and she enjoyed the attention. And when Jim tried medication to help him to have sex with her, she rejected him.

To give one more brief example, I counseled a self-deprecating woman named Katherine who grew up in a very strict Catholic household. Her parents forbade family members from talking about sex and stressed that "sex was for the married only." From puberty on, Katherine fought off urges to express herself sexually in an effort to conform to her parents' wishes and the wishes of her church and community; however, this was not without consequence. Although she was a forty-six-year-old wife and mother by the time she showed up at my office, Katherine was still having trouble fully enjoying sex with her husband. Unfortunately, Katherine's internalized *conformity vs. rebellion* master conflict prevented her from becoming comfortable with sex. Part of her wanted to enjoy physical intimacy, but the other side inhibited this guilty pleasure.

The take-home point here is that if you are thinking that the primary cause of your relationship troubles is sex, think again about whether or not those problems might actually be symptoms rather than the cause.

WHAT'S BEHIND YOUR FINANCIAL PROBLEMS: YOUR MASTER CONFLICT AND MONEY

Money always has been a close second behind sex as a troubling symptom of the master conflict. When couples struggle financially, it's easy to understand why they'd fight. But money conflicts can also stem from less obvious roots. For example, I once treated a couple whose combined annual income exceeded $300,000. Yet whenever Gordon, forty-nine, a real estate agent, bought something, Eleanor, fifty-two, an attorney, would scold him. Her initial defense: "I earn more than he does, so I should be in charge of how the money is spent. If Gordon wants more control, he can start earning more." Later in treatment, the real truth came out: Eleanor's father made a good living in his heyday, but he made a few terrible investments and lost most of his money and assets, leaving his family almost penniless when he became disabled and could no longer work. When her husband bought even the smallest item, Eleanor's anxiety level skyrocketed. "Once she yelled at me in a store, in front of several customers, because I was set to buy a couple candy bars," Gordon said, shaking his head at the memory. "She can get really crazy about money even though we have plenty."

1. ***Adequacy vs. inadequacy***—*When partners feel both adequate and inadequate regarding money matters.*

2. ***Control vs. chaos (Control vs. out of control)***—*When partners want to be in control financially but set themselves up to be financially out of control.*

3. ***Justice vs. injustice***—*When partners resist or protest unfair financial restrictions, yet create the need for them with their excessive spending or inability to set financial limits.*

4. ***Power vs. passivity***—*When partners are conflicted about possessing financial power. For example, one partner may demonstrate a desire for financial power by working hard to earn a lot of money, yet choose a mate with little motivation to earn, and vice versa.*

5. ***Success vs. sabotage (Big vs. small)***—*When partners are conflicted about succeeding and failing financially.*

To dive deeper again into an example, consider how the money problems of one couple I counseled, which were so severe that they were threatening their marriage, grew out of a *control vs. chaos* master conflict.

Annette and Troy were quite a contrast. Troy, a forty-four-year-old actuary, was a tall, thin, quiet man; Annette, a fifty-year-old dentist, was a five-foot ball of fire. Gesticulating with her hands, she spoke loud and fast: "I can't live like this," she told me. "He's so cheap, you'd think we're about to go into bankruptcy. Who needs this? I was single for many years, and I handled my finances just fine, thank you."

Troy was visibly distraught. He leaned forward in his chair, clasped his hands, and slowly shook his head from side to side. "I don't know what to do, Doc," he said in a soft voice. "Annette spends money like there's no tomorrow; and she shops at the most expensive stores. The other day she spent hundreds of dollars on food. That's insane." Annette's face turned red. "Wait a minute," she interrupted. "We were having people over for dinner, and I didn't have time to prepare anything because I got hung up at my office, so I bought some of the foods I thought our guests would like. Sue me." Troy looked at me and complained, "You see, this is the attitude I get. I can't control her, and she can't control herself. She also wants to send our daughter to a private school that costs about eighteen thousand a year. How can we do this if she spends the way she does?"

At face value, it appeared as though Annette was out of control and Troy was the practical one. That is, until Annette went on the offensive with a potent counterattack. "Why don't you tell the doctor about some of your toys?" she said. "You know . . . your taste for expensive sportscars and custom-made golf clubs. You worry me when you spend huge amounts of money at one time. I don't do anything like that. I wanted to put that money toward our daughter's education." Troy admitted that he sometimes spent more money than the couple could comfortably afford. The difference between the two: Annette spent in smaller, more frequent amounts; Troy bought big-ticket items. In a sense, both partners wanted to be in control, but both were out of it. By marrying each other, they both demonstrated a need for control and chaos.

Figuring out where Annette's master conflict came from wasn't that difficult because she grew up in a chaotic environment. Her father was a chronic philanderer who ultimately abandoned his family and never looked back. As Annette describes it, her father didn't believe in monogamy and disappeared when she was eleven.

Annette's mother *was* a responsible woman, but between her studies and her job, she spent little time at home. Annette said that she and her brother ran wild. "To this day, neither one of us likes to be told what to do," Annette admitted. Well, when I first met Annette she was still running wild and resented being told what to do. She knew that she was disorganized; even her dental practice was a mess—bills unpaid, insurance claims misplaced, phone calls unreturned. She also was addicted to chaos. She was exhilarated by her ability to do anything she wanted at any time. No restraints! And she resented Troy or anyone else who tried to stop her.

On the other hand, Annette craved control; she liked the security and comfort of Troy's practical nature. In fact, she once said that he kept her balanced. Her dysfunctional compromise to her conflict: allowing Troy to make decisions, as long as they didn't restrict her or interfere with her compulsive desires.

What about Troy's conflict? He grew up in a disciplined environment. "My dad was pretty strict and my mom was responsible," he said. "She was always on top of things. Dinner on the table at five every night, laundry cleaned and folded . . . you name it." While Troy admired and had modeled himself after them, he also resented their strictness, which ended up being rigid and suffocating at times. As an adult, Troy was attracted to Annette's freewheeling personality and all the excitement and chaos it brought. But her style also scared Troy, because he thought it would result in serious financial trouble.

PROBLEMS WITH YOUR PARTNER'S PARENTS: YOUR MASTER CONFLICT AND YOUR IN-LAWS

In-law problems have been a favorite subject of comedians and sit-coms, but when they're happening to you, there's nothing funny about them.

For many adults, their master conflicts render them unable to cope with their in-laws without making what are already quite difficult problems worse. The fact is that many in-laws do behave in ways that are extremely difficult to deal with. Four of these behaviors are the most common ones I've heard about from the couples I've treated, and for each of these, I will explore how a master conflict can make coping with them even harder.

Control and Manipulation

When in-laws attempt to take over their adult children's relationship by either direct or indirect means. In-laws who have trouble relinquishing control over their children may try to regain it well after their children are in long-term relationships or marriage. This often will evolve into a control struggle between the parents and their child's partner, who may feel that his or her power is being threatened. Some in-laws try to openly *bully* their children into conforming to their wishes. I once treated a couple whose in-laws insisted that they have dinner with them once a week, even though it was an undue hardship for their daughter-in-law, who worked full-time as an elementary school teacher and was raising three young children. While she tried her best to abide by her in-laws' wishes, if she missed one dinner, she was severely criticized for being disloyal to the family. Another couple I treated reported in frustration that their in-laws would show up at their house unannounced and take control over the child-raising. The in-laws constantly questioned their daughter's and her husband's parenting skills, and they managed to convince the young couple that if they didn't cede control to them, they'd do irreparable harm to their children.

Some in-laws are less confrontational but just as effective in getting their way. These people prefer an indirect, manipulative route to regain control over their children. Take, for example, Stan and Janice. Stan and his mother have always been close—probably too close. After his father died, they were inseparable. When Stan and Janice decided to marry, his mother freaked out. It's not that she didn't like Janice—she did. But losing Stan was just too much for her. She first tried to stop the marriage by doing a lot of crying and begging. When that didn't work, she tried some really manipulative things, like telling Stan that Janice was marrying him only for his money—which was ridiculous, because she had more than he did. She also called Janice's mother, started a fight with her, and then told Stan that Janice's mother had called her terrible names. She's not quite as bad now, but Janice refuses to let her in the house, which of course is causing Stan some big problems. He's become angry and sarcastic toward Janice and believes his wife isolated his mother so that Janice's mother can be the "one and only" grandmother to the kids.

Janice was making a point about Stan's difficulty with letting his mother down. He was, after all, a loyal son his entire life. When Stan's father died, Stan's master conflict (self vs. loyalty) really kicked into gear, causing him severe marital problems. How could he choose between taking care of his poor mother and his own marital needs? By itself, this was quite a dilemma, but Janice didn't help matters. While she demanded loyalty from her husband, by banishing her mother-in law she not only evoked more panic in her but more animosity and less loyalty from him. In other words, her *self vs. loyalty* conflict compelled her to overreact to her mother-in-law's separation anxiety, because it would someday guarantee that she would lose her husband's allegiance. Janice knew prior to marriage that Stan and his mother were close. If she weren't in conflict about how much loyalty she deserved, she probably wouldn't have married a momma's boy.

Intrusive

When in-laws uninvitingly pursue or infiltrate the lives of their adult children. Many in-laws are so interfering that they nearly destroy their children's relationships. Jason, twenty-seven, a newlywed with an entry-level job at a paint company, complained that his mother-in-law was an unrepentant meddler who took too much of his wife's time away from him. His story is relatively common.

> *The biggest mistake I've made in my life was to move within five miles of my mother-in-law. I should've moved to another country. She has no life. I think she calls my wife at least ten times a day, and she's at my house almost every night. Most of the time, she has nothing important to say, but she gets mad if my wife can't hang with her. I swear she spends more time with my wife than I do. You'd think they're married. The worst of it: my wife can't stop her. My father-in-law's probably glad she's always at my house.*

Jason was right about his mother-in-law's intrusiveness. But although his wife, Monica, agreed with his assessment, she refused to support him. Why? Because instead of gently confronting Monica about allowing her mother to absorb so much of the couple's time, he chose to repeatedly scold both her and her mother, effectively alienating both of them and enabling Monica and her mother to join forces against him. The couple's master conflict of *closeness vs. distance* turned out to be the underlying culprit. While Jason complained that his mother-in-law took Monica's time away from him, he helped create even more distance between himself and his wife through his volatile approach to the problem. While Monica admitted that her mother was overbearing, and that she wanted to spend more time with Jason when he wasn't raging, she encouraged her mother's intrusiveness—first by not setting limits with her behavior, and second by joining with her against Jason.

√**KEEP IN MIND: Dysfunctional adults usually have poor marriages, which may cause them to turn their full attention to their children's relationships. When adult children can't or won't set appropriate boundaries with their parents, their relationship will eventually suffer.**

Rejecting

When in-laws refuse to accept their adult children's relationships. Norm, sixty-three, never approved of his new son-in-law, Evan, a twenty-seven-year-old financial planner; he didn't think Evan was good enough for his only daughter, Heather, whom he always referred to as "my little girl." Heather claimed her father also objected to their religious differences: Heather was Jewish and Evan was Catholic.

Parents often respond negatively when their children enter into an interreligious marriage, so I understand Norm's position. But I met Evan, and he seemed like a very solid, stable young man. He certainly seemed dedicated to Heather. Nevertheless, because Norm couldn't talk his daughter out of the marriage, he decided to shun them both. Heather's is a typical situation. She says her dad has always been controlling, and he gets really angry whenever she doesn't do exactly as he wants. Marrying Evan upset him, and he launched a campaign against them. He never gives her any money and didn't attend the wedding. "My mom keeps telling us to give him time, but I feel like my marriage is running out of time. Evan and I are beginning to crack. I know he feels like an outsider. Last week Evan told me that maybe we should divorce and marry people with the same religious background."

Instead of standing strong as a unit against an extremely controlling father-in-law, Evan and Heather's *conformity vs. rebellion* master conflict was getting the best of them and destroying their marriage. Why this master conflict? Both partners knew well before their wedding date that Norm was against the union; they also knew that he was a powerful and controlling man, quite capable of being vindictive. And while they admit they knew they were going to be in for some grief if they married, their conflict compelled them to give Norm a run for his money. After all, both partners were generally rule followers, but the sign of their conflict is that whenever they did rebel, it was a whopper. This couple may just as well have been viewed as struggling with an *acceptance vs. rejection* conflict, but because of each partner's history of vacillating between conforming and rebelling, I went with that, and it seemed to resonate with the couple enough to help them.

Undependable or Unsupportive

When in-laws can't or won't meet the expectations of their adult children. Some in-laws are emotionally, physically, or financially incapable of lending support to their adult children. While many of these older adults are too selfish, others may be incompetent. Whatever the reason, those adult children with exaggerated expectations (caused by their master conflicts) are more likely to react to disappointing in-laws with anger and frustration, eventually fueling a cycle of battle. Maxine, thirty-seven, has an eight-year-old daughter, Elisa, with cerebral palsy; she feels strongly that her in-laws go out of their way to avoid helping her and her husband with her. Maxine knows it's her and Dean's responsibility to care for their daughter, but they need more help and can't afford to hire anybody permanently. "We've tried babysitters, but they can't handle Elisa. That's another thing; Dean's parents are athletic and in great shape. Plus, they're loaded—they could help us pay for child care." When she's challenged her in-laws on this issue, they say, "We're retired; we'll help in an emergency but nothing regular; it's too much work." Her husband hates their reaction, but he accepts it. He says that they've always been self-centered.

Handicapped children can be a handful, but Maxine had a point that even Dean couldn't argue with—his parents were pretty self-centered. Nevertheless, Dean and Maxine's master conflict of *justice vs. injustice* only made a bad situation worse. The source of Dean's conflict was easily traceable to his family of origin. He grew up with self-absorbed parents, and from this experience, he had developed an intense concern about fairness and obligation, which he demonstrated by being accepting about his parents' unwillingness to help out with Elisa, thereby fulfilling his duties faithfully.

Maxine's father disappeared when she was eight, and her step-father was a kind but incompetent drug addict who had trouble holding down a job. She described her mother as chronically depressed. Simply put, Maxine's parents were a great disappointment to her, and if Maxine wanted anything in life, she had to get it herself. For example, she took out massive loans and held down two jobs to put herself through college. This background caused Maxine to develop a *justice vs. injustice* conflict, which made it horribly difficult for her to accept the injustice of her in-laws' unwillingness to offer support. And this was true even though she knew that they weren't really dependable. Her master conflict caused her to minimize that issue so that she could focus on injustice.

Once again, let's take a more in-depth look at one couple's struggle with the exacerbation of in-law problems by their master conflict. Craig and Trudy's master conflict of *specialness vs. ordinariness* was responsible for an in-law problem that nearly destroyed their marriage. Craig's parents never liked Trudy, and she had become aware of that well before they married, and now, at ages forty-three and forty-two and after ten years of marriage, the issue was coming to a head. "They hate me," Trudy said in therapy. "And Craig won't stand up to them. He allows them to abuse me. They never wanted Craig to marry me, but for God's sake, we've been married for ten years and have three children. It's time to leave it alone. They're ruining my family." Craig looked at the floor and shook his head. "Yeah, it's no secret my parents didn't want me to marry Trudy. My mother really dislikes her. It's to the point now that they don't even speak." Indeed, Craig's parents were mean to Trudy. His mother refused to work on their wedding with her; now she doesn't return telephone calls and conveniently forgets Trudy's birthday and the couple's wedding anniversary. Craig's father refers to Trudy as "the Philadelphian," because she was born and raised in the city of brotherly love. An Arizona native, Craig met her while they were in graduate school in Colorado, pursuing their MBA degrees.

So why did Craig's parents, who were successful entrepreneurs in Arizona, loathe Trudy? Simple—they didn't think she was good enough for their son, and they would have preferred for him to marry a woman from a prominent family. Trudy's father was a postal worker and her mother a school secretary; it also didn't help that Trudy's parents were divorced.

While Craig and Trudy agreed about the severity of the situation, Trudy was right in saying that her husband lacked the nerve to stand up to his parents. His excuse: "They won't change. What's the use?" Initially, Trudy tried to please her in-laws by making regular calls and encouraging her children to maintain as close a relationship as possible—something she knew her mother-in-law would appreciate. But nothing softened their feelings.

Over time, as I worked with Craig and Trudy, it came out that Craig was the "superstar" of his family, and his parents hoped that he would one day eclipse their financial success. His two younger brothers eschewed college for the produce business, but Craig made it all the way through graduate school. He also was a star track and field athlete in high school and college. His good looks, boyish charm, and affable personality didn't hurt either, making him popular with women throughout his life. A former prom king, he admitted that he lived a charmed life: "My parents adored me. I could do no wrong. Even my friends noticed it."

Craig was the prototypical "golden boy," and once you experience this, it's pretty hard to give it up. Who wants to pass up such a great source of self-esteem? Craig certainly didn't. Nor did he want to stand up to his parents and risk losing his coveted position in his family of origin—even if his passivity was wrecking his immediate family. But there's also a flip side to Craig's conflict—his need for ordinariness.

It took awhile in treatment for Craig to figure out the origin of his partial need to be a regular guy, but we eventually discovered two major sources. First, Craig felt some lingering guilt for having been the favorite child, and he eventually dropped this on me: "I felt sorry for my two younger brothers. I think they could've done more with their lives if my parents had given them as much support as they gave me." The second source was harder for him to uncover. He actually had had some difficulty being the favored child, because he'd felt that he had to be perfect and tried to avoid disappointing his parents. He feared if he did, he'd lose his coveted position in the family. Also, Craig said he couldn't rebel or express any negative feelings, such as frustration or anger, because his parents would be especially sensitive to his emotions and shut him down. Craig likened his life to that of a celebrity who always had to be careful about how he behaved, lest he create a big sensation with even a minor indiscretion. "My mother especially would overreact to any mistakes or issues I had," he recalled. "My brothers were free to screw up any time they wanted. Don't get me wrong, I still liked being the favorite. I'm just saying it could be tough."

Trudy's story is different, but her master conflict ended up the same. Following her parents' divorce, she lived with her mother and regularly saw her father, who treated her like a "little princess." She said, "My parents hated each other, but they always put their differences aside if it was in my best interest. They gave me whatever I wanted. I think they were competing for my love and loyalty, but I was treated specially even before their divorce." And what of the other side of Trudy's conflict? Where did that come from? In therapy, Trudy eventually learned that she also felt uncomfortable and somewhat guilty that her parents vied for her affection. It was these internalized feelings that were mostly responsible for her need to be ordinary.

I hope this chapter and those preceding it have helped to make clear how master conflicts operate and why they are at the root of so many relationship problems. I am sure, however, that it is still somewhat difficult for you to put your finger on which conflict is probably at the core of your own relationship troubles. This is such a novel way of thinking about relationships that I fully expect that you will need more guidance about how to diagnose your own master conflict and exactly how and why it has gotten out of control. In the next set of chapters, I will provide you with step-by-step tools for digging into the story of your life and that of your partner, and for then applying the insights gained in order to diagnose which of the master conflicts that you earlier identified is really the one you should focus on.

6

PINNING DOWN
YOUR MASTER CONFLICT

Based on the preceding chapters and the exercises you've done, you may have already diagnosed a master conflict that you believe is at the core of the relationship problems you're having. But you might still be unsure whether a master conflict is really at play and which one it is. Determining which inner conflict may be at the heart of your issues usually isn't easy, and it's to be expected that putting your finger on it will take some hard work. In this chapter I will share some particularly helpful methods to use in order to either home in more definitely on a master conflict you're struggling with or confirm that you've made the right diagnosis.

In light of the new information you've gathered, I suggest that you go back now and review the answers you filled in for your exercises and, if needed, reassess what master conflicts you believe operate in your own life and that you have in common with your partner. Review the life experiences that may have led to your conflicts, as well as those you know of that might be root causes for your partner. Have these thoughts at hand as you then work through these additional diagnostics, and note that you may need to keep delving into your relationship and your life history and that of your partner over a period of time. Patterns of conflict in a relationship are usually difficult to discern, especially because revisiting arguments often reignite the pain and anger you experienced. Our life stories can also be painful to delve into, requiring us to confront family dynamics and events that we may have suppressed from memory. All of this probing is likely to provoke strong emotions regarding old grievances and unpleasant memories that you prefer to leave in the past. But I assure you that examining those emotions and letting yourself really feel them is one of the most powerful ways of not only identifying the conflicts at play in your life but also of coming to terms with them, so that you can more effectively manage them.

FIND YOUR CIRCULAR
RELATIONSHIP PATTERN

A good first step is to look for a "circular pattern" in your arguments with each other; a vicious cycle of contention to which you and your partner *both* contribute. You do something to get your partner upset. Your partner handles it poorly by yelling. Then you get annoyed with your partner for freaking out and find another way to upset him or her. Your partner then gets even angrier. It's one big Ferris wheel that keeps going around and around with no end in sight. This is a common symptom of a shared master conflict; you are rehearsing the same fight over and over because you both have an underlying need to be having it.

In my experience in counseling couples, if you do have a shared master conflict, then you'll have at least one major circular pattern that helps you maintain that master conflict. Either one of you can start the circular process on any given day. There's only one thing that's guaranteed—one of you will.

I suggest that you now write a description of the vicious cycle in your relationship. To help with that process, read the examples below. Notice the clarity and precision with which the circular patterns are described and try to be similarly specific yourself. Coming to this kind of crystal clear understanding of the nature of your out-of-control arguing can be enormously helpful in realizing that there is something deeper behind your struggles than the particular complaints that set each of you off. Keep in mind that although most of the examples use "husband" or "wife," the patterns are not gender-specific, and you should try to see how each situation might apply.

- *My wife says she wants me to tell her what's on my mind. But every time I try to speak, she interrupts me, usually with a criticism. So I give up. Then she gets mad at me for shutting down.*

- *My wife is very sensitive. She says she wants me to tell her how I feel about our relationship, but she cries every time I mention something that bothers me. I decided a long time ago to stop telling her about anything that I'd like to see changed. Now she accuses me of being distant.*

- *My husband can't have a serious discussion without making a joke of it. It aggravates me, so I walk away from him and nothing gets resolved. Then he tells me he can't talk to me because I have no sense of humor.*

133

- *My husband gets mad and raises his voice when I try to talk to him about our marriage problems.* He has such low tolerance! I'd rather talk to my friends about my problems—and I do. Then he gets upset because I tell "outsiders" what's going on.

- *My partner says she wants to talk about problems as soon as they happen.* But she always brings up the past every time we talk. I feel bombarded, so I stop talking altogether—which she throws in my face the next time we fight. I gave up a long time ago.

Okay, so now that you have described the particular circular pattern for you and your partner, it's time to delve deeper into what is really behind these reactions to each other. Before delving further into the methods that I recommend for definitively diagnosing whether a master conflict is at the core of your problems and what it is, though, I should address the issue of whether to do that on your own or with your partner. There are many ways to do this. You may want to work first on your thoughts about your own master conflict independently and then begin discussing your insights with your partner, or you and your partner may be comfortable working simultaneously. In the latter case, you can still work separately on your diagnoses and then share them, or you can work together every step of the way. One of you might forge ahead faster than the other, and in that case, I urge you to be sure to give the other time to catch up. Make sure that you don't turn the project into a control struggle of its own, with the partner who has moved further along badgering the procrastinating partner to catch up. Keep in mind that one of the keys to successful couples therapy is to keep the partners as emotionally close as possible during treatment. If one person gets too far ahead of the other, the relationship can suffer. So even if you decide to first do your own diagnosis and only then talk about it with your partner, be sure that you give your partner the benefit of coming to his or her own conclusions, and maintain an open mind about differences in perspective between you. If you can keep your discussions truly exploratory and stay receptive to insights from each other, you are much more likely to come to a satisfying diagnosis of your relationship issues and arrive at a good resolution of them.

EXAMINE YOUR FEELINGS

An important next step in this process of deeper probing is to focus on the feelings you have about your relationship, and particularly on what is most upsetting and provoking for you. I know that concentrating on those feelings is painful, but in order to solve your problems, getting in touch with your feelings—especially the ones you experience repeatedly—is vital. Suppressing emotion won't bring you true security or stability. If you suffer from anxiety or depression, for example, it's crucial that you not ignore those symptoms. Both are scary and painful, but they're also valuable signs that something deeper is operating. One of my former professors once told me that people with anxiety have trouble getting rid of it, because they rarely put the time into figuring out what caused it in the first place—they either suffer with it or take medication.

The subject of medication is important here, especially considering that many people experiencing relationship problems go on medication to relieve their anxiety and emotional distress, or to help them get to sleep. Doing so can be enormously beneficial, and I want to be perfectly clear that I'm not against medication. Indeed, many studies have shown that the best treatment for emotional problems is a combination of medication and psychotherapy. But people sometimes also use medication as a fast fix or as a means of treating the symptoms rather than the disease. If a master conflict is at the root of your problems, using medication to mask your symptoms of distress may only allow your inner conflicts to thrive, and your symptoms will usually return as soon as you stop taking medication. There are situations in which medication is crucial; if you have not been able to experience joy in your life for some time, or you're feeling nearly immobilized, or of course if you're suicidal, you need to get psychiatric medical treatment, and you should do so right away. But if you're experiencing less severe anxiety or depression, or other common feelings that result from relationship problems, such as anger or sadness, I want to encourage you to let yourself really feel those emotions. I suggest that you actually write them down, because doing so can be a powerful way of helping to articulate them and will allow you to revisit your thoughts about them as you go through the rest of these exercises.

Then think hard about what is triggering those emotions, not only in your relationship but also outside it, in the rest of your life. What really sets you off? What things that your partner says or does are most provoking to you? In what other areas of life do you often feel the same way? You may want to write down your thoughts about these questions also and reflect back on these answers periodically as you work through the following exercises. Making the connection between your distress and its causes can be tricky, but when you do, it can be eye-opening.

For some people, identifying the emotions that arise from their relationship problems might be difficult, because these emotions may be suppressed. If this is true for you, then you may well find that you have physical symptoms that take the place of emotional expression. If you are experiencing any persistent physical symptoms—headaches, tics, sleeping problems, stomach distress, lower-back or neck pain, to name a few—think about whether it might be possible that they are related to your relationship problems.

Take the case of my client Charlene, a forty-four-year-old married woman who was averaging about three panic attacks a week; she even had one while driving. I recommended that she try medication, and that took the edge off her anxiety, but it was the exploratory work of examining her life deeply that helped Charlene find the actual source of her anxiety. When she asked herself what she was thinking about, or what was happening in her life, just before her attacks, she discovered that the answer was that she was dreading going to work; the thought of it made her want to run away. By then delving into why she was feeling so strongly about work, she figured out that her attacks were related to a conflict she felt about continuing to work with her husband, Tom, in their family-owned business, transporting older folks to doctors' appointments. It was Charlene's dream to go back to college and finish her pharmacy degree, but she felt terrible about her fantasy because she knew Tom would be upset; she saw him as a decent guy and didn't want to abandon him. Charlene was trapped by guilt, yet she resented working in a business she hated. Her severe anxiety was a symptom of this dilemma. So far so good; Charlene had identified the immediate cause of her emotional stress.

The next step in identifying a master conflict that might be at work is to connect the emotional distress you're feeling to previous circumstances in your life. Ask yourself whether you consistently lived with these feelings in your family of origin and also in your past intimate relationships. One of the important features of a master conflict is that it causes the same distinctive set of feelings whenever it is triggered, no matter how much time has gone by. Making the connection to previous experiences that triggered the same emotions will help you identify what underlying conflict may be causing that distress.

In Charlene's case, when she asked herself if she ever felt anxious in the same way in her family of origin, she realized she had a lifelong conflict about doing what people wanted her to do rather than exercising autonomy over her life. Her parents were very conservative and controlling. She loved them but never felt free of their rules, especially the ones that limited her social life. To gain some independence, Charlene rebelled—first by quitting college, then by moving in with a boyfriend. She had fought hard for her freedom. But she also paid heavy consequences: Charlene suffered her first panic attack at age eighteen, and her parents punished her by shunning her.

Charlene realized that she had also felt the same kind of anxiety in her past romantic relationships, and by probing into what had caused that anxiety, she saw that she had a weakness for obsessively controlling men. She began to understand that she had a powerful inner conflict; part of her wanted to do as others told her to do, and was searching out controlling types, but at the same time she greatly resented those attempts to control her. She then realized that she had been rebelling in her marriage for this same reason. Though, to all appearances, Charlene was a shy woman who rarely outright provoked fights, she had been rebellious, or what is often referred to as passive-aggressive, with Tom. She often showed up late for work and forgot her driving routes regularly. Tom complained every time she failed to do her job, which was causing a great deal of strain in their marriage, but he didn't suspect that she wanted out of the business.

Before this, Charlene hadn't seen her rebellious streak; she was in touch only with her obedient side. By connecting her current feelings to her past, she uncovered the deeper truth that she was suffering from the strains of a *conformity vs. rebellion* master conflict. After coming to this realization, she was able to speak candidly with Tom about her career ambitions. And though, as expected, Tom wasn't happy with her desire to leave the family business, he gave her his blessing to return to school. Tom was a good man, and he didn't want to see his wife suffer. He also appreciated the simple truth that Charlene would likely undermine the business eventually with her rebellions if she didn't follow her dream.

Take some time now to see if you can similarly connect your current life situation, and the problems you're having in your relationship, to your prior life experiences, and you may also gain clarity about what master conflict might be at the root of your distress. So, first:

- ***Identify your feelings.*** *Remember that all feelings are important, so try not to push them under. If, for example, your husband constantly criticizes you, ask yourself whether you feel angry, anxious, depressed, disappointed, hurt, sad, or inferior. You can have all of these feelings at once (and more), but try to identify the one or two strongest emotions. Acknowledging your feelings will no doubt be easier for you if you grew up in a home where you were allowed or even encouraged to express yourself without consequences. But if you came from a "closed* *family system," where you were ignored or punished, you will have to work that much harder to allow yourself to feel. In this case, give yourself "permission" to feel. And remember, you're an adult now . . . you're in charge . . . there is nothing to fear anymore.*

- **Get specific.** *Ask yourself how you feel about your current relationship problem and whether you ever "felt" like this as a child or with past lovers. Though Charlene was easily able to identify her anxiety, she was shocked to find that she had the same feelings growing up in her family of origin. This suddenly clear connection really helped lead her to her master conflict.*

CHECK FOR OVERREACTIONS

Another powerful means of homing in on your conflict is to think about times when you overreact, maybe flying off the handle in anger or breaking down in tears, when, if you think about the circumstances with the distance of dispassionate analysis, that reaction really wasn't called for.

An overreaction works like a reflex. You can't control yourself. You're compelled to react. Some people get angry, while others overreact by becoming depressed or sobbing uncontrollably. An overreaction doesn't have to be a big explosion. Simply put, it's a reaction that doesn't fit the crime. Such intense reactions are often the result of experiences from your youth that can help you identify the source of a master conflict. For example, if your father verbally abused you when you were a kid, maybe calling you names or putting you down regularly, you may have developed a *justice vs. injus-*

tice conflict. As an adult, this conflict increases the odds that you'll overreact whenever you think your partner—or anybody else for that matter—is mistreating you. Or perhaps one or both of your parents was emotionally distant, which may have caused you to develop a *closeness vs. distance* conflict. In this case, you might overreact by becoming angry when your partner doesn't tell you what he or she is doing when going out for a few hours to run an errand.

You don't have to be treated exactly the same way you were in your childhood to cause the overreaction in adulthood; the slightest hint of unfairness or disrespect may set you off. A little later I'll give examples of some typical situations in the lives of couples that provoke overreaction, and point out the master conflicts that are responsible.

Try to think about times when you have to admit to yourself you probably overreacted to something your partner said or did, and also about times you've done so in other areas of life. I suggest that you list them. You may be reluctant to characterize your reactions as extreme, and in that event you should list occasions when you had a strong reaction to something your partner said or did and then try to step back from them emotionally and ask yourself whether you were on target or over-the-top. Work hard to be honest with yourself, and keep in mind that all of us overreact sometimes; it's human nature. You should also include times that you know your partner thinks you overreacted, even if you disagree, or you might ask them to tell you about times that they thought you did. Be sure to ask *why* your partner thinks your reaction was extreme. You may not get an objective answer—after all, it's difficult for both parties to be objective about emotional conflict—but you might get valuable information. It's vital in these conversations not to get defensive. Listen intently and evaluate the information for logic and accuracy. Then compare it to your own assessment.

Now, in examining your list:

1. ***Identify what made you overreact.*** *What did your partner say or do to trigger your response?*

2. ***Think back. Have you always overreacted to this trigger or any trigger similar to it?*** *Try to come up with a few examples. If you can't remember what has set you off in the past, ask your partner for input.*

3. ***How did you overreact?*** *What specific feelings did you experience and/or express? Describe them fully; I suggest writing down the descriptions.*

Now, to help you connect those extreme reactions to an underlying master conflict, I have grouped below the master conflicts that in my experience most often provoke the major emotional overreactions. Put a check next to the feelings you usually experience when you overreact. You can check more than one feeling, but try to focus on the one you experience the most. Then, check the master conflict listed under the feeling that you think, from all of the analysis you've done so far, best accounts for why you overreact that way. For example, if you get enraged most often when you feel you're being treated unfairly, check the *justice vs. injustice* conflict. If you experience anxiety when someone distances from you, put a check next to the *closeness vs. distance* master conflict. You can check more than one master conflict, but you should try to see if you can identify one that is dominant in your overreactions. This will be important work as you continue to narrow down conflicts to the one at the heart of your worst relationship issues.

OVERREACTION CHECKLIST

Anger or Rage____

Adequate vs. Inadequate____

Because one side of you feels that you're an adequate, competent person and the other side of you believes you are an inadequate, incompetent person, any attack or perceived attack on your level of competence can result in an angry overreaction. For example, something as seemingly small as your mate's innocently questioning whether or not you'll soon receive a salary raise might, to you, imply that you're not earning an adequate living. Or, if your partner criticizes your outfit before going out to dinner one night, you may become livid, thinking that your ability to dress appropriately is in question.

Conformity vs. Rebellion____

If you have this conflict, one side of you wants to be conservative and traditional while the other side is attracted to a more liberal lifestyle, free of traditional boundaries and restraints. So, being forced to conform in your relationship might trigger an angry, rebellious overreaction. For example, you're likely to react in anger if your partner demands that you give up your career as an artist to seek a more stable, conservative desk job, even if you're having trouble paying the bills.

Giving vs. Withholding____

In this conflict, one side of you has a desire to give to others while the other side withholds. So, an angry overreaction might be triggered if you feel you give too much to your partner, or if your partner gives you little in return. The woman of a couple I treated flew into a rage anytime her partner failed to send an immediate text message reply validating his love for her.

Justice vs. Injustice____

With this conflict, you have a strong desire to resist or protest unfairness and injustice, yet another side of you helps create it. A rage can be triggered from even the slightest sense that you are being treated unfairly by your partner even if you set yourself up to be taken advantage of. The man of a couple I saw was extremely angry because his girlfriend didn't voluntarily put his name on her mortgage once he moved into her house. Sharing his conflict, the girlfriend reacted with an equal amount of rage to what she felt was a grossly unfair demand.

Self vs. Loyalty____

Here, one side of you wants to choose your own path in life and follow your dreams while the other side of you feels that you must remain loyal to your parents and not stray too far from their lot in life or what they might want for you. An angry overreaction can erupt if you think your partner is making you choose between him or her and something that you perceive would be disloyal to your parents. For example, if your partner demands, against your parents' wishes, that you quit your career and move with him across the country, rage can be triggered before, during, or even long after the move.

Person vs. Object____

A side of you wants to be treated as a respectful human being while the other side believes you're unworthy of this treatment because you aren't perfect. Partners with this conflict set themselves up to be treated as objects and then can explode with anger when it happens. I treated a couple in which the woman never allowed her husband to celebrate their anniversary. She said it was a needless waste of money. Yet when her husband followed her instructions and did nothing special for their twenty-fifth anniversary, she was furious. She couldn't believe he had the nerve to treat her this way. "I'm a human being," she screamed.

Power vs. Passivity____

In this conflict, one side has a strong desire for control and power, while the other side wants to be free of the responsibility that comes with being in charge. An angry overreaction can be triggered when you perceive that your power is being challenged, when you're feeling too controlled, or when you're feeling burdened by too much responsibility. The man of a couple I once treated got extremely angry whenever he thought that someone was asking him to do something he felt they could handle themselves or that he felt was a waste of his time. He once snapped at a woman for asking him to take charge of one of their children's sporting events.

Specialness vs. Ordinariness____

One side of you has a need to feel special, to set yourself apart from others, while the other side of you believes yourself to be ordinary or "less than." An angry overreaction tends to occur when you perceive that you're treated by your partner as an ordinary person, no more special than anyone else. I once saw a married man in individual therapy who was having a long-term affair. Oddly enough, this man got extremely angry when he found out that his lover was going on vacation with her husband. He strongly believed that if he were truly special to his lover, she would never go on a trip with her family, even though he did it all the time.

Trust vs. Distrust____

Because in this conflict one side of you is trustworthy and the other side isn't, you might fly into a rage at even the slightest hint of deceit, no matter how harmless. The wife of a couple I saw flipped out when her husband mistakenly underestimated—by only a couple of dollars—how much he had paid for a new shirt.

Anxiety____

Closeness vs. Distance____

If you have this conflict, you want to be close to someone but on the other hand you feel more comfortable connected from a distance. Overwhelming anxiety can be triggered when you feel either too close or too far away. A woman I treated individually would experience great anxiety when her boyfriend talked about moving in with her. But she also felt anxious when he traveled abroad for work.

Commitment vs. Freedom____

Similar to *closeness vs. distance,* in this conflict a side of you desires the stability and security that a commitment can bring while the other side wants to be free of restraints. Extreme anxiety can be triggered when you're considering solidifying your relationship, as well as when you are free but alone. I treated a woman in individual therapy who had panic attacks whenever the man she happened to be dating at the time spoke of marriage. But she also experienced a great deal of anxiety when she didn't have a man at her side.

Control vs. Chaos (Control vs. Out of Control) ____

A side of you prefers peace, order, and control while the other side is attracted to uncontrollable drama and chaos. You'll most likely experience much anxiety when you feel out of control. But you may feel the same when you are under control, for fear the control will soon somehow be taken away from you. You may fool yourself into thinking you're bored without drama, but boredom is sometimes a cover for a lurking anxiety. I treated a man individually who was in a wonderfully stable relationship with a woman who loved him with all her heart. While this man recognized his partner's goodness, he began an affair with a woman who turned his world upside-down. Both relationships made him anxious.

Security vs. Risk____

One side of you fears risk and prefers being cautious in life, while the other side craves the excitement of risk. Similar to *control vs. chaos,* you may experience acute anxiety when you take even the smallest risk, but you become bored with too much security. Again, the boredom may be anxiety in camouflage. In couples therapy a man I saw freaked out when he found that his wife invested some of their money in a relatively safe money market fund. But, even though he had more money than most people he knew, he constantly worried that he would someday lose it. This same man set an astronomically high goal to reach for his retirement savings. He believed that he would feel secure only when he had 4 million dollars saved. At the time I treated him he had saved close to 3 million dollars.

Success vs. Sabotage (Big vs. Small) ____

One side of you wants to be a success, and the other side of you sabotages this success. This is a tricky one. If you have this conflict, the more success or failure you have, the more anxiety you experience. In fact, you may very well overreact with extreme anxiety to even the smallest successes, by making them bigger than they are. Or, you may exaggerate your failures and experience over-the-top anxiety. I'll never forget the couple I saw who seemed to get more and more anxious the wealthier they became. It got to the point that they began to take turns sabotaging each other's careers in order to reach a more comfortable balance to their conflict. In reality, they achieved only what was appropriate for their levels of education and their work ethics.

Depression or Hopelessness___

Acceptance vs. Rejection___

One side of you needs to be accepted and approved of, but the other side questions your worthiness. If you suffer from this conflict, you can overreact with a grave sense of hopelessness or depression if you perceive yourself as being rejected. Real or imagined, your reaction might be the same. I treated a single woman who took even the slightest criticism about her so seriously that she eventually needed an antidepressant. In some cases her dates would simply be joking with her, but it didn't matter—she treated all remarks with the same level of seriousness. At one point she felt so hopeless that she gave up dating for a couple of years.

Adequacy vs. Inadequacy___

In this conflict one side of you feels competent and the other side feels incompetent. If you suffer from this conflict, it can be pretty easy to get overly depressed when you perceive that your level of competence is being questioned. The man of a couple I treated became paralyzed with depression when his wife expressed concerns about their financial situation. True, the partners were struggling, but I believed he took his wife's comments far too personally.

Satisfaction vs. Disappointment___

A side of you feels comfortable and satisfied, while the other side is in a state of chronic disappointment or dissatisfaction. It is easy to overreact with depression if you suffer from this conflict. The wife of a couple I treated went from rags to riches during our treatment process, but no matter how far she'd come, there was a part of her that was disappointed in herself and her spouse.

Frustration and Helplessness___

Resolution vs. Misery___

Part of you wants to resolve your problems and be happy, while the other part blocks resolution and remains in a state of misery. There's frustration galore with this conflict. The solutions are usually staring a couple in the face but the partners can't resolve whatever problems they've got. I treated a man whose wife told him point-blank in couples therapy that she loved someone else. But, rather than move on with his life, this frustrated man continued to try for several years to make his relationship work, while his equally trapped wife continued to cheat on him rather than cut herself loose. Both partners made themselves martyrs.

Guilt___

Getting Your Needs Met vs. Caretaking___

One side of you wants to meet your own needs and at times put yourself first, but the other side needs to be selfless. This one is easy. Caretakers tend to overreact with guilt when they take care of their own needs. They can feel even guiltier if they put themselves ahead of their partners. A woman I treated by herself expressed guilt and remorse whenever she couldn't make her daily trip to see her husband in an alcohol rehab clinic. Quite an overreaction, given that the clinic was several miles from her home, she was ill herself from diabetes, and she had to take care of her children and her sickly mother.

Conformity vs. Rebellion____

People with this conflict can overreact with guilt over even the slightest form of rebellion. I once treated a woman who was upset with herself because she had sexual fantasies about men other than her husband. She felt that her fantasies were a form of cheating and she came to see me by herself to help her stop them.

Legitimacy vs. Illegitimacy____

A side of you feels authentic and valuable, while the other side believes you are an imposter or fake. Believe it or not, if you have this conflict you might overreact with guilt if you're being treated too well by your significant other. Being treated as having value may stir up guilt if you see yourself as less than worthy of such attention. A man I saw individually who was adopted as a child always viewed himself as illegitimate. He had trouble believing he was worth much and as a consequence he would dump any woman who truly wanted him. He always seemed to overreact to any little thing wrong with them and then get rid of them. And the nicer they were to him, the greater the guilt he felt and the quicker he put a stop to the relationship.

Self vs. Loyalty____

In this conflict, anytime you go against your parent's wishes you run the risk of experiencing some guilt. However, the amount of guilt you experience is usually disproportionate to what you've done or wish to do. I treated a couple who fought furiously because the husband wanted his wife to get a job. Though the wife wanted to work, she experienced tremendous guilt because her traditional mother kept telling her that a "good mother" stays home and cares for her children.

Hurt___

Acceptance vs. Rejection___

The hallmark of this conflict is that you may overreact with hurt to any form of rejection. Even when your partner offers constructive criticism, you may take it as a rejection and experience great emotional pain. A woman I once saw with her husband was extremely hurt because she felt that his suggestion that she get a job was a rejection of who she was—a homemaker. The husband claimed that he wasn't unhappy with her, but that he was drowning in bills and could use her help. He actually went out of his way to tell me how intelligent she was, but this proclamation didn't do much to soothe his wife's hurt.

After completing this exercise, look back at the three master conflicts you identified as your top picks at the end of chapter 2 (pages 60–62). You may well find that one or two of them come up consistently. If so, you should take some time now to try to connect that conflict to your experiences growing up and to past relationships, and then look at the troubles you're having in your current relationship in light of this pattern. If, for example, you have determined that a *justice vs. injustice* conflict seems to be at the heart of many of your worst overreactions, go back through your life history and try to put your finger on what might have caused you to have this conflict. In doing so, go back to the Family of Origin Impact Test, the External Life Impact Test, and the Family of Origin Trauma and External Life Trauma lists that you filled out at the end of chapter 3 (pages 89–92). These should serve as useful guides for zeroing in on the conflict that is most dominant in your current relationship.

ALSO CONSIDER UNDERREACTIONS

If you are a person who is given to underreacting rather than over-reacting, the previous section may not have resonated with you all that deeply. What do I mean by underreacting? Well, some people hardly react even when major things happen in their relationship. A stark example is when one partner is having an extramarital affair and the other isn't reacting to the obvious signs. I've treated my share of people who fail to ask their spouses where they were and whom they were with at odd hours of the night. One woman I counseled told me she would return home from a rendezvous with her long-term lover at 3 or 4 a.m., and her husband never questioned her whereabouts. I've seen women not question their husbands even after they discover that they've sent definitely suspicious emails to other women. This is a form of denial, and it can also be a sign of a master conflict. Take, for example, the case of Bridget, who came to see me to decide whether to stay married or run off with her married lover.

At age forty-four, after seventeen years of marriage, she had been having an affair for nearly five years with the same man—her boss, Marshall. A medical equipment salesperson, she was confident she'd never be caught . . . and she was right. Because of her job, Bridget was able to travel with Marshall all over the state on business—and share his hotel rooms. You'd think her husband, Corey, a forty-five-year-old contracts officer, would suspect something. After all, Bridget was rarely home and she rarely had sex with him.

It turned out that this couple shared the master conflict of *specialness vs. ordinariness.* When she was growing up, Bridget had been treated in her family as special by one parent and ordinary by the other. As an adult, she couldn't bear to think of herself as an "ordinary" wife and mother, and over time, in therapy, she admitted she had a compelling need to feel special. Marshall met that need by constantly showering her with gifts and compliments—he worked hard to make her feel as if she were the only woman on earth. He also let her know that he wanted to have sex with her all the time. He could be very demanding, too. He would object when she spent time with her husband. But Marshall had no intention of leaving his wife, and this meant that there was no risk that their relationship might evolve into the ordinary. This dual life was exciting for Bridget in many ways but also exhausting and at times humiliating as well. She was working overtime to replicate her family of origin.

What about Corey? Why didn't he object to all the time Bridget spent at work? And why didn't he pick up on what must have been signs that she was having an affair with Marshall? Well, in his family, his parents never made him feel special. Bridget's neglectful attitude toward him fulfilled his need to feel ordinary. As for his need to feel special, he fulfilled this by being highly self-involved and obsessive about his career. The main reason Corey didn't pick up on Bridget's extramarital activities was that he was narrowly focused on his own career and hobbies. He always took work home and was absolutely driven to keep getting promoted. Most of the little spare time he had was devoted to his second love, community theater, and he rarely spent time with the couple's ten-year-old twins. By focusing on himself, Corey was able to make himself feel special, and his underreaction to Bridget's lack of attention supported him in maintaining his conflict. If she hadn't made him feel so ordinary, he would have felt less reason to treat himself as special.

Howard, thirty-eight, was quite the underreactor in his nine-year marriage to Janine. Even though Janine rejected him sexually for nearly two years, Howard refused to confront her. His response: "I want my wife to have sex with me, but I don't want to pressure her. I believe she'll come around in her own time because deep down she really likes sex."

Howard's rather passive stance in the face of a potentially serious marital symptom startled me, and it also confused his wife. But what really stood out was his failure to ask the kinds of questions a partner in his predicament would ask a mate, such as, How long do you think this problem is going to last? Are you having an affair? Are you still attracted to me? Do you want a separation or divorce? Instead, Howard minimized his wife's lack of sexual interest in him and continued to be the model husband in an effort to gain her favor. And, ironically, it was Janine who pushed for treatment. She was worried that she would never regain her lust for her husband and that she was wasting time being married to him.

While Howard's underreaction was strange, it was put in perspective by his family history. His mother, divorced and single, was an angry, highly critical woman who was never satisfied with her son's performance. "If I got one B on my report card she would complain," Howard said. "If I brought home a date who wasn't a beauty queen, she would put me and my date down. I wanted to please her, but nothing worked." From this, Howard developed an *acceptance vs. rejection* conflict, which he replicated in his marriage. He then continued to support his conflict by underreacting to his marital symptoms.

Janine also suffered from an *acceptance vs. rejection* conflict. She too came from a family in which she struggled to please her parents. And, despite being a model child—athletic, beautiful, brilliant, and very pleasant—she was never able to gain their favor. Her conflict was reflected in her history of falling for men who rejected her, only to reject their acceptance of her. The difference between Howard and Janine is that Janine wanted to tackle her conflict, and Howard wanted to shove his under the rug, so to speak. Soon I'll give more examples of typical situations that have provoked underreaction in relationships and their associated master conflicts.

To figure out whether or not you might be underreacting due to an inner conflict, take a look at the list of situations below. Put a check next to the ones that apply to your relationship and that you think you have most consistently underreacted to. For example, if your partner won't get a job, and you've said little or nothing about it, put a check next to "partner refuses to work." You can check as many situations as you'd like, but again try to focus on the one or two to which you underreact most frequently. Next put a check after the master conflict listed beneath the situation that you think is responsible for your underreaction. Again you may check more than one master conflict, but do try to focus on the one or two you think fit best.

UNDERREACTION CHECKLIST

Partner Had or Is Having an Affair___

Commitment vs. Freedom___

In this conflict, one side of you desires the stability and security that a commitment can bring, while the other side wants to be free of restraints. If you underreact to your partner's affair, it could be because underneath it all you're not committed enough to the relationship to want to save it. You might even be unconsciously and passively encouraging your partner to leave you. A woman whose husband had been cheating on her for several months said to me in an individual session, "I hope he runs off with his girlfriend—they deserve each other."

Justice vs. Injustice___

If you have this conflict, one side of you has a strong desire to resist or protest unfairness and injustice, yet the other side of you helps to create it. If this is the case, you may consciously or unconsciously be passively encouraging your partner to have an affair so that you can feel the injustice. In this sense you're making a quiet martyr of yourself.

Resolution vs. Misery___

In this conflict, a side of you wants to resolve your problems and be happy, while the other side blocks resolution and remains in a state of misery. If you underreact, particularly to a long-term affair, then you probably suffer from this conflict because you desire on some level to be miserable for a long time to come. I've treated people in this situation and, despite many viable alternatives, they plead helplessness and remain miserable—sometimes for years.

Power vs. Passivity___

A side of you has a strong desire for control and power, while the other side needs to be free of the responsibility that comes with being in charge. If you underreact to an affair, then you are rejecting the power side of your conflict and embracing the passive, powerless side.

Specialness vs. Ordinariness___

On the one hand you have a need to feel special—to set yourself apart from others—but on the other hand you believe yourself to be average or ordinary. If you underreact to an affair, you're making a statement that the "not so special" side of you is dominant and that anyone can take your place. I treated a man individually who had this philosophy. One side of him felt as if he had value, but in explaining his feelings about his wife's affair, he said in a nonchalant tone, "It just goes to show you, nobody is that special." His confusion about his specialness made it difficult for him to get angry.

Partner Is Not Having Sex with You___

Acceptance vs. Rejection___

You want to be accepted and approved of, but the other part of you questions your worthiness. If you underreact to a sexless relationship, you might be suffering from this conflict because you're allowing yourself to be rejected. I treated a man individually who allowed his wife to have very infrequent sex with him despite that fact that he catered to her on every level. His reason for his nonchalant attitude: "Long ago I accepted the fact that my wife is far more attractive than I am. And that she was never as attracted to me as I am to her. But I know I could never get anyone even close to her in the looks department, so I'll live with what I have."

Adequacy vs. Inadequacy___

You may recall that in this conflict one side of you feels that you're an adequate, valuable person, while the other side believes that you are inadequate. If you underreact to a sexless relationship, it might also be a sign that you're conflicted about your adequacy or level of competence. You might not feel attractive enough for your partner, as was the case in the preceding conflict, or you might feel as though you're an inadequate sexual partner. You may be more likely to underreact in this situation if you suffer from sexual performance anxiety or have a physical problem that seriously affects your sexual prowess. Why complain and stir up more trouble when you can hide from even bigger issues? A man I saw by himself refused to make an issue out of his sexless marriage because he knew that he had rapid ejaculation problems and he wasn't yet willing to deal with them.

Closeness vs. Distance____

You want to be close to someone, yet another side of you feels more comfortable connected from a distance. If you underreact to a poor sex life, then you might be conflicted about getting too close to someone. The man of a couple I treated insisted on maintaining a separate residence from his longtime girlfriend, in part so that he could control the number of times they had sex. His reasoning: "The more I sleep with her, the closer she expects me to be, and I'm not ready for that yet."

Satisfaction vs. Disappointment____

A side of you feels comfortable and satisfied, while the other side of you is in a state of chronic disappointment or dissatisfaction. If you underreact to a poor sex life, you might be conflicted about satisfying yourself. After all, what could be more pleasurable than a great sex life?

Giving vs. Withholding____

One side of you has a desire to give to others, while another side of you withholds. If you underreact to a skimpy or nonexistent sex life, this could be because you're in conflict about allowing yourself to receive. As in the preceding conflict, you may be passively encouraging your partner to withhold from you.

Resolution vs. Misery____

If you live with a long-standing dysfunctional sex life, this conflict may be the culprit. As you probably know by now, it has a habit of trapping people in miserable situations for inordinate amounts of time. I've treated unconsummated marriages as well as couples who were stuck for up to fourteen years in sexless relationships.

Partner Works Very Little or Refuses to Work____

Conformity vs. Rebellion____

One side of you wants to be conservative and traditional, while the other side is attracted to a more liberated lifestyle, free of traditional boundaries and restraints. You might underreact to a partner having work difficulty because of a rebellious side of you that bucks tradition. The wife of a couple I treated only mildly protested her husband's refusal to work, in part because both partners claimed to be upset about the amount of taxes they were paying when he was employed.

Satisfaction vs. Disappointment____

If you're in a relationship with someone who barely functions, and you refuse to do much about it, you could be unconsciously trying to disappoint yourself. I've warned several people in premarital therapy about this issue, but most proceed full steam ahead.

Justice vs. Injustice____

I treated a woman in couples therapy who tolerated her husband's refusal to work because, like him, she felt anger toward his former place of employment for laying him off. Both partners felt that they suffered a grave injustice, given that the man had worked at his company for eighteen years.

Self vs. Loyalty___

A side of you wants to choose your own path in life and follow your own dreams, while the other side feels that you must remain loyal to your parents and not stray too far from their lot in life or what they may want for you. You may underreact to your partner's inability to function because you do not want to hurt him or her or apply too much pressure. You'll be particularly susceptible to the conflict under these circumstances if your parents experienced financial difficulties and you felt sorry for them. I treated a woman who felt so sorry for her out-of-work husband that she took on two menial jobs to make up for his. Her reasoning: "I saw my father go into a deep depression after he lost his job. He could never work again. I'd rather have my husband happy than like that."

Success vs. Sabotage (Big vs. Small)___

One side of you wants to be a success while the other side of you sabotages this success. If you have this conflict, it wouldn't be unusual for you to underreact to your partner's financial failure, since a part of you is attracted to failure. As icing on the cake, you might even unconsciously help your partner sabotage their career. I can't tell you how many people I've seen who persist in breaking up the relationship when the partners are on the verge of their greatest achievements. This is a beautiful attempt at sabotage. I've even treated spouses who have gone to their partner's company parties, gotten drunk, and created a scene that could have cost their partner's promotions or in some cases their jobs. Even just underreacting to your partner's success is a way to reduce both of you. I treated a man in couples therapy whose wife would react with a droning and indifferent "That's nice, dear," no matter how much success he achieved. The man told me that her reactions broke his spirit.

Partner Spends Too Much Money___

Control vs. Chaos (Control vs. Out of Control)___

In this conflict, one side of you prefers peace, order, and control while the other side is attracted to uncontrollable drama and chaos. Under-reacting to a free-spending partner is a surefire invitation to chaos. I treated a woman who simply could not set limits with her spending. Though her husband complained mildly in couples treatment, he continued to give her blank checks. It was only when he realized that she was getting them deep into debt that he finally cut up her credit cards—a move that eventually cost him his marriage.

Legitimacy vs. Illegitimacy___

A side of you believes yourself an imposter or fake while the other side feels authentic and valuable. You may underreact to your partner's spending habits if material things make you feel more legitimate. There are plenty of people out there who feel good about themselves only through the acquisition of "things."

Security vs. Risk___

One side of you fears risk and needs to be cautious in life, while the other side craves the excitement of risk. If you underreact when your partner spends like a drunken sailor, then it might be because you're getting off on the risk they are taking. You might even use it as permission to take your own risks.

Success vs. Sabotage (Big vs. Small)___

You might underreact to your partner's exorbitant spending habits if you have a stake in their failure. What better way to sabotage success than to allow your partner to get both of you in deep financial trouble? The wife of a couple chronically overspent and ran up all her credit cards even when she knew her husband was trying to get his business out of debt.

Partner Abuses or Humiliates You___

Legitimacy vs. Illegitimacy___

If you feel illegitimate or flawed, you may underreact to being abused. A man who consistently allowed himself to be taken advantage of by his abusive fiancée came to tell me his story. Adopted as a child, he was neglected by both his biological and adoptive fathers, and felt that he had to put up with more because he was literally illegitimate.

Resolution vs. Misery___

It can be very difficult for many to escape an abusive relationship. But you may underreact to abuse because you're in conflict about whether or not to lead a life of misery. I treated one woman by herself who, despite being beaten several times, stayed in her marriage. In fact, when she came too close to getting up the nerve to leave it, she dropped out of therapy instead.

Person vs. Object___

A side of you wants to be treated respectfully as a human being, while the other side believes you're unworthy of good treatment. If you suffer from this conflict, you may underreact to being abused because you're not quite sure whether you're a human being or deserve to be treated like one. I've treated my share of erotic dancers, porn actresses, and prostitutes over the years, and they all treat themselves and the men in their lives as objects. Most of these women were treated this way in their childhoods and they expect no more if and when they settle into a serious relationship or marriage.

Partner Uses or Abuses Drugs or Alcohol___

Getting Your Needs Met vs. Caretaking

In this classic scenario, one side of you wants to meet your own needs and at times put yourself first, while the other side of you needs to be selfless. Some caretakers underreact to their counterpart's addictive behaviors because they themselves are addicted to caretaking. And on some level this means they are in conflict about having a healthier partner who can function independently. There is no shortage of stories about caretakers who leave the relationship only "after" their partners have cleaned themselves up.

Control vs. Chaos (Control vs. Out of Control)

If you underreact to an out-of-control addict, you may be suffering from this conflict, because there's nothing more chaotic than an addict on the rampage. You never know what's going to happen next. Will your partner sell the furniture for drug money? Will your partner get drunk and cause a serious car accident, hurting him- or herself or others? Will your partner be able to hold down a job? Endless worries and sleepless nights will give you all the chaos you can handle if you don't tackle a problem like this head-on.

Now look back again at the three master conflicts you identified as your top picks at the end of chapter 2 (pages 60–62) to see what degree of overlap there is with this list. Then take some time to try to draw connections between these underreactions and your experiences growing up. If you have underreacted to your partner spending too much money, and you checked off *security vs. risk*, for example, now you can explore the family situation that you believe led to this conflict about the degree of risk you want in your life. Then consider how that may have played a role in your attraction to previous partners, and then connect those insights to the problems you're having in your current relationship.

WATCH FOR CONTRADICTORY AND IRRATIONAL BEHAVIOR

Perhaps the most helpful clues that you can use to zero in on your master conflict are instances in which you and your partner act in self-contradictory ways. Why? A conflict is sort of a contradiction—two sides battling and being contrary—and this often shows up in people acting two ways at once.

There are three types of contradictory behavior: (1) *communicative/verbal;* (2) *action-oriented;* or (3) *a combination of communicative/verbal and action-oriented.* A communicative or verbal contradiction is just what it sounds like: a partner says one thing and then follows it with the complete opposite. For example, a husband may flatter his wife by praising her intelligence and soon after call her an idiot. An action-oriented contradiction is a bit trickier. It occurs when a partner physically acts one way then follows it with the opposite. For example, when I was in college, I took a girl to the movies who snuggled up against me but froze up when I put my arm around her. Fearing I was being intrusive, I took my arm away; she then immediately put her arm around me. I didn't know what to make of it. And a contradiction in communicative and action-oriented behaviors can be absolutely baffling. This is when one partner physically contradicts a verbal comment or vice versa. A wife may *say* that she wants more sex with her husband but *physically* rejects him when he tries to please her. Or a wife may kiss her husband then yell at him when he kisses her in return.

An important point is that a contradictory action or comment can come either immediately following the action or comments it's contradicting, or somewhat later, in a sort of a delayed reaction. This can sometimes make it harder to convince a partner that she or he has actually been contradictory or can make it seem that the contradiction was inadvertent, a matter of having forgotten about what was said or done earlier. Don't let this fool you. A good way to assure yourself that you are really identifying contradictory behavior indicative of an inner conflict is that it is repetitive. You should be seeing it over and over. If it happens once or twice, it may not be significant.

Let's take a look at one couple I counseled who exhibited the sort of contradictory behavior that should be a red flag. Courtney was a forty-three-year-old high-school guidance counselor, and her husband Jared, fifty-three, was an appliance store manager. Courtney angrily complained that Jared never initiated any conversations with her and that "living with him was like living alone." But when Jared tried to speak, Courtney interrupted him with a barrage of complaints and criticisms, in effect scolding him, while she leaned on the edge of her seat and pointed a finger at him. It got so intense that at one point I thought Courtney might throw the tissue box at Jared. What did Jared do? He sat passively looking at his shoes and saying nothing. What do you think happened next? Courtney went ballistic, because Jared had shut down. And there is the glaring contradiction. Did Courtney want Jared to engage her or not? Answer: both. This way her conflict could live on. Through her contradictory behavior, Courtney was demonstrating the most common master conflict, *power vs. passivity*. She wanted Jared to be assertive, but she was afraid to allow him to wield any power.

Meanwhile, Jared also contradicted himself. He complained that his wife was too bossy and demanding; he also said that he had no power—that is, no voice in the marriage—and that his opinion didn't matter. Yet as soon as Courtney interrupted him, he shut down and gave up—essentially turning all the marital power over to her and allowing her to dominate him. Jared had the same *power vs. passivity* conflict. He wanted more power, but not enough to assume responsibility in the relationship. For Jared, it was easier to live as if he were in a trance.

Here is an example of a contradiction that's both communicative/verbal and action-oriented contradiction. Renee, forty-eight, a high-school administrator, came to see me with her husband, Tony, fifty-two, who owned a restaurant. Renee complained about Tony's lack of sexual interest in her, and revealed that they hadn't had sex in two years. Tony replied, "I'm still attracted to Renee; in fact, I think she's beautiful. I'm just mad as hell at her for spending too much money. She's like a sailor on leave. She buys anything and everything, especially clothes. It seems like a box is delivered to our house every day from some mail order catalog. We have three credit cards that are maxed out. I think I'm responsible for only about two thousand, and that was for a car repair. I'll tell you this: If she won't stop spending, I won't sleep with her—*period*." Ignoring Tony, Renee looked at me and said, "Money's not the real problem. Besides, he spends money too. And even if it was, what man punishes his wife by withholding sex? That's sick. Guys don't do stuff like that." Sounds like a real standoff, doesn't it? The funny thing is, apart from this issue, Renee and Tony were one of the most loving couples I'd ever treated. Not only did they compliment each other often, they also did something few couples in therapy do: they hugged and kissed at the end of every session. It appeared as though they gave to one another but drew the line when it came to money and sex.

After only two treatment sessions, Renee began to pressure me to prescribe some sex therapy exercises. I didn't think they'd work, but Renee threatened to fire me unless I added this component to their treatment. Thinking it might prove my point about their relationship problems, I convinced Tony, after counseling him alone a few times, to initiate sex with Renee. "Someone has to break the struggle," I explained. "Besides, think of all the money you'll save." Tony was skeptical but finally agreed to give it a try. "Anything to prevent going bankrupt," he mumbled, half-jokingly. The plan was for him to approach Renee on the upcoming Friday night.

Well, the night came, and Tony did his part. As Renee lay in bed, Tony made his move, kissing her passionately and wrapping his arms around her. But Renee turned him down. "I'm a little tired tonight," she said. What? It was only 8:00. And guess what? In another week, Renee started complaining all over again about her poor sex life. What Renee *said* she wanted she *physically* rejected. This contradiction helped lead me to the couple's *giving vs. withholding* master conflict. Both partners complimented each other frequently and demonstrated affection outside the bedroom. They also enjoyed socializing together. But they took turns withholding sex.

Irrational behavior comes in the same three forms as contradictory behavior: communicative/verbal, action-oriented, and a combination of the two. Now, for the most part, I have some pretty sharp clients. I don't hear a lot of crazy or irrational statements from them. But once in a while, I'll hear something ridiculous, and I sit up and take notice. Take the sweet, loyal, caretaking Lillie, whose husband, Rick, was addicted to prostitutes. Lillie was distraught about the whole situation, but when I asked her whether she was still sleeping with Rick, she looked at me as if I were speaking Greek. "Of course," she said. What about using protection? A straight-faced Lillie said that she didn't think she needed to, because Rick had assured her that he always used condoms with the prostitutes. This was outrageous. It was bad enough that Lillie had continued to be intimate, but how could she trust that her husband was telling her the truth about using condoms? Under the circumstances, Lillie needed to protect herself against a sexually transmitted disease. Taking note of how irrational her reaction was, I eventually was able to help them see that they had a *person vs. object* conflict. Lillie wanted to be treated like a cherished wife, but by marrying an addict and enabling him to continue his addiction, she ensured that he'd treat her like an object. As for Rick, being with prostitutes allowed him to satisfy the object side of his conflict, and being with Lillie satisfied the person needs.

Taking note of any sort of behavior by one or the other partner is a remarkably powerful method for tracking down their root inner conflict, even if at first that behavior seems entirely unrelated to their relationship problems. Consider this story of one of the most unusual and fascinating examples of irrational behavior I've encountered, which ultimately led me straight to the couple's master conflict.

Dale, fifty, claimed he was depressed and useless, because he was struggling at his job as a salesman and would probably soon lose his job. When he spoke, he kept his eyes trained on his shoes, and he spoke in a gentle and tentative voice. What I found most interesting about Dale, though, what really stuck out, was the way he handled his favorite hobbies: violin, golf, and photography. Dale wanted to enjoy and be competent at these activities, but instead of practicing or taking lessons, he simply collected expensive equipment and instruments that he rarely touched. At the time I saw him, he had several violins, the best golf clubs made, and an assortment of cameras. I thought this oddity was important to explore, even though Dale and his wife both thought I was wasting their time in doing so.

While Dale's wife, Jan, thought his behavior was "a little odd," she didn't consider it vital to their marital issues. But I believed Dale's spending so much without learning how to use these things was an important symptom. Eventually we came to the conclusion that they both were under the sway of a *success vs. sabotage* conflict. Dale demonstrated his competence and ability to be successful by knowing everything about his equipment and by always purchasing the top of the line. However, he also made himself feel incompetent—or sabotaged his success—by never learning properly how to use these acquisitions. For her part, Jan was conflicted about her level of attractiveness and her career issues.

Go with your gut in exploring whether a contradictory or irrational behavior that you or your partner engages in is related to a deeper conflict. If you have the slightest hint that something's off—that something doesn't make sense or fit—pay attention to it. It may ultimately not be related to an inner conflict or to your relationship problems, but investigating whether or not there might be a link will always be worthwhile. If you're wrong, you can always apologize. If you're right, you may be able to prevent further damage to your relationship.

EXAMINE YOUR MASTER CONFLICT OUTSIDE YOUR RELATIONSHIP

Another powerful method of pinning down your master conflict is to look beyond the struggles in your relationship. You probably demonstrate the same conflict, to some degree, at work and/ or with friends. A man who gives and withholds from his wife will most likely be inconsistent in the way he treats his colleagues or employees at work. If this same man has a conflict about conforming in his relationships, he may at times be rebellious at work. A woman who caretakes her partner will probably overwork for friends.

In this step, your assignment is to look outside your relationship to see whether you act the same with others or whether others treat you the same way that you're treated in your romantic relationship. This is a great way to help solidify the identity of your master conflict. It's harder to recognize your conflict in all the different contexts of your life. But when you can, you'll be much better for it.

Note that when you look for your master conflict outside your relationship, you don't need to find a perfect match in behavior. There might be one, but most of the time the fit is less than exact. For example, you may be staying in a job even though your boss unjustly refuses to give you a promotion and you have every reason to expect you could get another job. The comparable situation at home may be that your partner is withholding love and affection and you are not demanding more. To see how conflicts outside a relationship can be so instructive about those at play within a relationship, consider the case of Perry, a perfect example of a guy whose master conflict operated both at home and at work.

Perry was a smart man. I first met him and his wife, Susan, in marital therapy, and they decided to stop therapy before they had really gotten to the bottom of things. A few years later, Perry came to see me alone to talk about his job situation. I remember well his opening remarks: "Steve, I don't want to talk about my marriage. I want to spend my time talking about my problems at work. Okay?" I was forewarned, which of course made me extra suspicious that things weren't going well at home, either.

For several sessions, I listened to Perry complain about his unsupportive boss and the incompetent men who worked under him. His boss didn't argue with Perry's complaint that his sales force was incompetent, yet he also didn't support him by offering to make some changes. With more conversation, I discovered that Perry's boss had told Perry that he didn't like the way Perry treated his employees—a fact that came out in a confrontation between them. It became clear to me that Perry's boss disliked Perry's critical management style. And this led me to make a connection with his marriage. Perry's wife had said that she felt he treated her with disrespect. "He talks to me like I'm a loser—like I'm an idiot. That's no way to talk to your wife," Susan had said with anger in one session. Fortunately for this couple, Perry was able eventually to accept the connection and they both started marital therapy, discovering in that process that they suffered from an extreme *justice vs. injustice* master conflict.

Take some time now, if you still aren't sure of what master conflict you should be focusing on, and think about where else in your life you are having conflict. See if you can identify any underlying similarities. This can be a powerful way of bringing the nature of your conflict into sharp focus.

CHECK WITH YOUR SIBLINGS

One last method I can suggest for pinning down what master conflict may be ruling your life is to consult with your siblings. Earlier I told you that siblings may have different master conflicts. But they may also share yours, and even if not, they may have valuable perspective on your family life that can help you zone in on the way in which you are conflicted and why. What if you don't speak with your siblings? It's certainly not unusual for battle lines to be drawn in a family. Family dynamics tend to take their toll, and most siblings find it almost impossible to be objective. Some have aligned with Mom; others with Dad. As you might expect, children of divorce are even more prone to form what we therapists call "coalitions." And, believe me, it's hard to talk civilly about the family of origin to a sibling who's in the other camp. Unfortunately, the reality is that some siblings downright hate one another.

I once treated a forty-five-year-old woman who couldn't forgive her younger brother for being favored by their father. Even though more than thirty years had passed, she still hated her brother and refused to speak to him. He made multiple efforts to repair the relationship damage, but she wouldn't consider making peace.

Whether you're completely estranged from your siblings or you're an only child, I recommend that you contact the next closest relative—the one most familiar with your family of origin. If you're cut off, you may want to reach out first to a close aunt or uncle. If you're an only child, go to a godparent first and then a close cousin or one of your parents' best friends. Just make sure you've chosen reasonable people, not people with obvious axes to grind. The downside to this alternative is that whomever you choose will not have experienced your family of origin precisely the way you and your siblings did. The upside is that you'll probably get a more objective opinion. As an only child, I went to my godmother, and the visit was very productive. Here are some tips you can use to interview a sibling. With a bit of adjustment you can use them to gather information from friends and relatives as well.

- *Initiate contact in person if possible. It's harder to be rejected when someone's looking you in the eye. If your sibling lives too far away, use the telephone. Too many misinterpretations happen when emailing; it's also more difficult to convey accurate feelings with this mode of communication.*

- *Be vulnerable. Admit to your sibling that you're struggling with a problem. You don't have to be specific, but by leading with vulnerability you're more likely to evoke empathy.*

- *Be gentle in your approach. It's important to remember that a discussion of the family of origin may raise a significant amount of anxiety in your sibling. You're probably not the only one who has unresolved issues.*

- *Ask key questions. You only need to ask a few specific questions, such as: What did you think of our father? What did you think of our mother? I have a conflict that's been causing me some distress; can you relate to it? The answers should give you some insight and let you know whether you and your sibling are on the same page. You may even learn that your sibling has experienced similar problems in his or her life or relationship. Never pressure your sibling to give you the answer you want, and make sure you pace your questions, leaving time in between each one. If you bombard your sibling, you're more likely to raise their anxiety level and put them on the defensive. You might also end up with a very brief consultation. You'll fare better if you create a relaxed atmosphere.*

- ***Avoid becoming defensive.*** *Sidestep potential control struggles. If things get heated, pull back until calm is restored. Try not to offer your opinion until you get a feel for how your sibling perceives things. This may help you avoid engaging in a coalition battle or control struggle. Your sibling may try to get you to choose sides, but remain objective, like a good journalist. Remember, you're doing research, not advocating for a cause.*

- ***Remember that your perspectives don't have to be exactly the same to be helpful.*** *Take what you can get and be happy, because probing the past isn't easy.*

- ***Let your sibling know that their perspective was very important to you.*** *Empathize with their position.*

- ***Send the message that you'd like to be able to talk again in the future.*** *Make sure your sibling knows that you would be available if they ever feel the need to initiate further discussion on the topic.*

The last step in analyzing what your master conflict is and how it's been affecting your relationship problems is to examine why it has gotten out of control. As I wrote in the first chapter, your master conflict was likely a strong bonding force when you first met, and if you had managed it well for years, then both of you probably had your conflict under relatively good control. It was not dominating your life, causing the sorts of problems that we've seen can result, such as self-sabotage at work, deciding to have an affair, or getting yourself into serious debt. A couple in which both partners' conflict is relatively well controlled is likely also to be able to manage the stresses and strains that the conflict inevitably causes in their relationship. But now it's gotten unwieldy and is leading to worse and worse fighting and/or other symptoms, so it's important that you examine what may have caused it to get out of control.

This is the time to take a close look at circumstances that may have changed in your life lately, or in your partner's life, and to analyze how the changed situation might have thrown your management of your master conflicts out of whack. To help you do this, revisit your answers to the External Life Event Impact Test and the External Life Trauma List on pages 91 and 92. Both instruments contain important information concerning significant work and family experiences that you may have had or are currently going through, such as whether you've lost your job, whether you or your partner has become seriously ill, and so on. While neither test is exhaustive, hopefully the questions will get you thinking once again about how your past may have influenced your internal conflict. Feel free to include any changes you think have had or are having an impact on you and your partner. It's best to consider any change at all in your lives, and let yourself think out of the box about this, because that change might seem on the surface like a good thing, or in fact be a good thing—say, you or your partner got a big promotion, or your partner has begun to be more openly affectionate. But remember: If you have a conflict about that good thing—maybe a *success vs. sabotage* conflict or a *closeness vs. distance* conflict—these positive changes will likely be causing you distress.

Once again, if you have uncovered a change in your lives that you think might have triggered your master conflict to rage out of control, go back now to your diagnosis of what you think your master conflict is and reflect on why this change would have caused you or your partner—or both of you—such discomfort, and in particular try to connect this change of circumstances with your diagnosis of things in your family life that caused you similar distress. And also look once again to see if you observe this same dynamic at work in prior relationships.

I hope that these methods of probing into your life and relationship will help you arrive at a firm understanding of your underlying inner conflict and whether it is playing an important role in your life and in your relationship problems. By becoming aware of your inner conflicts and the conflict that has been dominant in your irritation with your partner, you can develop keen insight into the ways in which your partner shares that same conflict and why it has begun to get out of control. As he or she goes through the same process of self-diagnosis, whether on their own or in ongoing collaboration with you, differences in views are almost sure to arise, and as I said earlier, it's vital that you both keep open minds about the realizations you are coming to and about each other's views. If you do come to agreement about a master conflict that is at the root of your problems, the next step is for you and your partner to decide how you are going to act on this knowledge.

Remember that it is nearly impossible to eradicate a master conflict totally. But for most couples, learning to manage it better, being empowered by knowing that it's at play, and accepting that it will always be a feature of their lives and their relationship can prove almost as effective. Just the knowledge of a master conflict can go quite far in deescalating the tensions it causes. For other couples, the best resolution may turn out to be ending the relationship because they determine that the way in which a master conflict has bonded them is unhealthy and they want to find a more satisfying relationship, which is not premised on that unhealthy bond. In the next chapter, I will help you think more deeply about which of these choices is best for you.

7

MANAGING YOUR MASTER CONFLICT, OR MOVING ON

As the ancient saying goes, knowledge is power. For many of my clients, the process of uncovering their master conflict and what has caused it to get out of control is in itself very empowering. The knowledge of their conflict enables them to counteract their impulse to become irritated with their partners. And the diagnosis of the circumstances that caused their conflict and of those that tend to cause the conflict to flare up allows them to identify when their conflict is taking charge so they can consciously regain control over it. This certainly isn't a magical process; learning to gain control over your conflict takes considerable work and persistence. But if you and your partner can come to agreement about the role that a master conflict has been playing in your lives and in your relationship problems, you will be in better shape for asserting control over it. This has been true for many couples I've counseled.

If you have not already started couples therapy but have come to the realization that you are struggling with a shared conflict, you might find that going into therapy at this point would be a good idea. The grip of these conflicts on us is tenacious, and the process of probing further into their nature and into your family and relationship histories through the rigorous approach of therapy can be enormously helpful. For one thing, it can relieve some of the tension of discussing the issues with your partner—helping to counteract the powerful defense mechanisms we discussed in chapter 4, which can wreak havoc on your attempts to grapple with your conflict. The therapeutic process can also greatly help in clarifying your diagnosis of how your family experiences have created your conflict, and can give you a structure for working to gain a new control over it.

Whether or not you decide to go into therapy, however, you can be making good use of your newfound knowledge on a daily basis in working to address your relationship problems. Whenever you have a fight or become angry or are hurt by your partner, tell yourself to consider right away whether your master conflict is to blame. Work hard to make yourself examine your emotions; then try to connect the situation that is setting you or your partner off to your diagnosis of the life situations that caused each of your conflicts.

Take Warren and Karen, for example, who were able to avoid having a big fight by calling to mind their master conflict. Warren, a fifty-three-year-old internist, and his wife, Karen, a housewife, had made great strides in treatment to uncover their *justice vs. injustice* master conflict, and for the most part they had gained control of it, having realized how it was behind so many of their fights. Sometimes it still threatened to rear its ugly head, though. Warren recounted one such episode in which Karen called him at work several times and really didn't have anything important to discuss. Karen defended herself: "I miss him and I like to check in once in a while." Warren said it happened repeatedly, and after the fourth or fifth call, he caught himself getting angry with her; he was really busy and his stress was mounting. "But instead of telling her off like I used to, I jumped to my injustice conflict and realized that I felt I was being treated unfairly. When I put it to her that way, things didn't get blown out of proportion." Karen smiled. "Yeah, I saw it," she said, "and I was proud I didn't respond by feeling that he was being unfair to me."

Of course, this process is not at all easy and you will inevitably still find yourself losing control regularly, at least for some time. But even in those instances, if you can revisit later the argument or the episode that caused you pain or anger and come to see how your master conflict was at play in it, you will develop a better and better ability to recognize the symptoms of this dynamic in the heat of the moment.

In order to build up your ability to interfere with the unconscious power of your master conflict:

- *Acknowledge the amazing power of your master conflict.*
  If you don't, you're more likely to end up revictimized. A little fear of, and respect for, your master conflict will help you control it. Pay particular respect to its elusiveness and remember that it is able to deploy a variety of defenses to block you from realizing that it's the real culprit behind your problems.

- *Never forget that your master conflict is always with you.*
  Keep it in the forefront of your mind at all times, because you never know when you'll need to tap into it to get yourself out of a jam. One technique you can use to make sure that your master conflict is accessible: Whenever something upsets you or doesn't

seem right, slow down or stop what you're doing for a minute or two. Then ask yourself whether your conflict is flaring up.

- **Whenever you experience a problem in your relationship, consider your master conflict the number one suspect.** *I'm not suggesting that every problem is caused by your master conflict, but because many are, it's the best place to start.*

- **Give yourself pep talks.** *If you believe that your master conflict is about to gain an edge on you, tell yourself that you know the master conflict may be at play, and that you're not going to allow it to rule you.*

This self-coaching can be quite effective. A few years ago, I treated a thirty-five-year-old trial lawyer who, despite a moderate amount of success in therapy, continued to struggle against his *success vs. sabotage* master conflict. Prior to treatment, he was sabotaging his marriage and career simultaneously; this caused the couple great emotional and financial stress. One of the exercises I assigned him was to step into the men's room right before he entered the courtroom and look himself in the mirror. Like a mantra, he was to then say to himself: "I'm going to be big today. Today I will be successful. I won't allow my master conflict to rule me in court." He told me that the exercise worked like a charm.

- **Consult your partner.** *If you and your partner have agreed about the role that a master conflict is playing, it may work well for you to mention to your partner when you begin to fight that your mutual master conflict may be operating. Of course, there may also be times when this will be only more irritating, but* *explicitly acknowledging the role your conflict is playing can be quite effective over time.*

- **Stay mentally strong and fight hard to stay healthy.** *It takes strong will to fight off a master conflict when it tries to gain control. You have to "hate" the symptoms you experience when your master conflict is in control of your relationship.*

- **Stay confident.** *If you fail to block your conflict's power or you fear that you're backsliding in getting control over it, don't panic and think it's the end of your relationship or that your master conflict will always get the best of you. Be positive. Remind yourself that you now know a good deal more than you did before about yourself, your partner, and the causes of your troubles. And remember to consider that it is inevitable that your conflict will still sometimes get the better of the two of you, but the key is that over time, if you keep working at it, this is likely to happen less and less.*

If you and your partner determine that you would like to better manage your inner conflict, I encourage you to make the effort, because this can ultimately lead to a happier, more satisfying relationship and a happier life all the way around. But there's no doubt that the process is emotionally wrenching, and if you do determine that this is your goal, then I strongly advise that you go into therapy. Probing into your past and your feelings about your family in the ways that will be required can be almost overwhelmingly painful; and it's best done with professional guidance.

In order to truly control a master conflict, you must attack it at its roots, and that can be as painful as getting a tooth extracted if not more so—trust me. You have lived with your conflict for so long that it has become very firmly embedded. Trying to yank it out simply won't work. The gentle process of trying to manage it is far more realistic, though it certainly isn't pain free. You must expect to go through a good deal of discomfort, and actual loss, if you are to truly control your conflict. You may have to acknowledge that your parents were right about you regarding some criticism they made that hurt you. Or you may have to prove them wrong in a big way and lose some of your admiration for them. You'll also need to allow yourself to experience disturbing feelings that you may have tucked away for years.

In order to reap the benefits of therapy, you'll need to buckle down and commit to the process of self-examination for the long haul. If you can tolerate the process, you'll be better off in the long run. And even if along the way your relationship fails, which it could, both you and your partner will gain knowledge and insight to start over in a new relationship that will be healthier. Let's take a look at a couple who were willing to pay the price for long-lasting health, and how they managed to stay together and come to a much more satisfying resolution of their relationship problem.

Andy, forty-five, and Becky, forty-five, suffered from a *closeness vs. distance* master conflict. When they first came to see me, they were dating steadily and lived separately but near each other; both were divorced. They claimed they wanted to marry but admittedly found a variety of ways to avoid consistent closeness. Becky suddenly developed low sexual drive, and they constantly bickered over the smallest things, such as who would wash the dishes. On vacation, Andy and Becky got along fabulously, but they'd start arguing just as they were about to return home or soon thereafter. It was a brilliant yet unconscious way to maintain their distance.

They came for treatment because both said they wanted to marry and they couldn't figure out a way to stop fighting.

It took a while, but once Andy and Becky uncovered their true master conflict, they had to make "the" decision, and it was unanimous: They chose to get control of their conflict and to shoot for closeness. Both said that they were in too much pain to maintain the status quo. Given their ages and their relationship histories, they felt this was their last chance to be in a loving, solid relationship. They also loathed the constant fighting and knew most of it was over minutiae. By the way, that's what you need to be successful in this option—a sense of desperation. Without desperation, it won't be worth it to you to go through the tough process of change.

Okay, so Andy and Becky had made up their minds. Now what? As expected, their master conflict put up a good fight for at least a year. The couple moved in together and set a wedding date, but they eventually broke up and called off the marriage. Let me tell you, it was some battle, but in the end, they came out victorious. We know what they gained, but what did each have to relinquish besides some space?

Becky always felt that her father was a wonderful man, primarily because he let her do whatever she wanted as a child and never criticized her. She had to let go of her fantasy of him as a great father, because in reality, he let her do what she wanted because he wasn't invested in parenting. In other words, he didn't care. Becky saw him as the "good guy" when she compared him to her controlling mother, a woman she described as a "witch." Becky feared the traumatic task of facing who her father *really* was and finally giving her mother credit for at least caring about her. By viewing her family of origin from this different perspective, she mourned the loss of the father she never had and dealt with the guilt she'd suffered over thinking that her mother had been awful most of her life. Becky cried a lot during these pivotal sessions, but in the end, it allowed her to draw closer to Andy. Instead of seeing Andy in the role of her controlling mother and unlike her easygoing father, she finally viewed him as more loving than her father, because Andy acted as though he cared.

Meanwhile, Andy faced the fact that his father was a selfish man who'd put himself ahead of his wife and son. He eventually came to understand just how controlling his father had been and how, as an adult, Andy grew to fear being controlled by a woman. More important, since Andy's mother died when he was young, he needed to accept how much this event has influenced his inability to get close to a woman for fear of losing her. He mourned all over again for his mother—and the kind of father he never had. True to our conflict theory, both Andy and Becky wanted closeness but feared it as well. It was comforting and dangerous at the same time, because it left them stuck somewhere in between—and living separately. I remember the frightened looks on their faces as they were going through therapy. I'm proud that they withstood the process and were able to draw closer rather than continuing their previous dynamic of "committing from a distance."

You and your partner may well decide that taking on your conflict in this way is just not realistic, or it may be that one of you is up for the job of working on your conflict but the other is not. Don't despair. In these cases, there are a number of ways that you might come to a new resolution about your relationship, any of which can yield perfectly valid results.

You may, in essence, agree to disagree. One of you may decide to accept that your partner is not going to change, and you may reach a compromise about your relationship problems. Just consider that if you choose this option, your master conflict demands that you take even less than what you want—it plays "hardball." But that may well be a deal that you're willing to accept given the circumstances of your life and relationship.

Take, for example, Esther, sixty-three, who was furious that her husband Harold, sixty-six, who was battling severe Parkinson's disease, had cheated on her several times during their forty-year marriage. They shared a *person vs. object* conflict. Although Harold's infidelities had stopped twenty years ago, the recent accidental death of their eldest child—the one who didn't get along with Harold because of his cheating—caused Esther's rage to bubble up. She was now struggling mightily to forgive her husband; she was even threatening divorce. Harold said that he loved Esther and regretted that he'd been unfaithful as a young man. "I was sick— probably a sex addict," he admitted. Harold apologized repeatedly, begging Esther to let him make it up to her. What's more, he even turned to religion and psychotherapy as a sign of his commitment to their marriage. No matter, Esther had enough anger to last a lifetime, and there was no indication that her anger would ever subside. Their therapy dragged on and on, with Esther raging at Harold for his past indiscretions and Harold pleading for a resolution. Harold wanted to work in depth on their conflict, but Esther wasn't up for that.

Looking haggard, Esther came to see me for an individual session. She said that being stuck was causing her a great deal of stress and she needed to make some kind of decision about what to do. We discussed whether she thought she could commit to a process of trying to get as much control over their conflict as possible, but she said she thought that was "too much work," and that she didn't think she'd ever completely forgive Harold, because she was "too disgusted and distrustful of him." It took about a month's worth of individual sessions with Esther, but she finally decided that she would stay with Harold and take care of him as long as he continued to be faithful and treat her as a human being, not a sex object as he had done in the past. Esther took divorce off the table, but she also vowed that she'd never have sex with him again, and she gave up the hope that she will ever be "in love" with another man. Romance would be sacrificed in the compromise; she and Harold would live as friends and traveling companions.

Esther believed that leaving Harold in his depleted health was too harsh, and she felt that giving up their comfortable lifestyle and becoming single again at her age was far too great a price to pay for another shot at love. So she opted to maintain her financial security and stability by staying in the marriage but would also keep emotional distance from Harold. It was the only way she could live with him somewhat comfortably. When Esther called me a couple of years later to refer a friend for therapy, she reported that she was staying true to her decision—and remained satisfied with it. Harold's disease stabilized, and the couple used a portion of their retirement fund to keep busy with their own individual hobbies and to travel the world together. Life wasn't perfect. But it was acceptable for Esther. Harold wasn't nearly as satisfied, but he got used to it. And he was happy that he no longer had to worry about the threat of divorce hanging over his head. In the end, the couple didn't go as far in their treatment as Andy and Becky did, but they did gain more control over their conflict than they previously had, and this turned out to be good enough for them.

I also treated a couple, Irving and Adrienne, who were both in their late fifties. Adrienne, a travel agent, dragged her husband into marital therapy, because she was unhappy with his appearance. Irving, who'd made a small fortune in the garment industry, had gained more than one hundred pounds during their twenty-six-year marriage. He wasn't unkempt, and he wore his expensive clothes well. But I could see Adrienne's point. The man she'd married was half the size of Irving, and over the years she'd gone to great lengths to keep herself fit and trim. Though Adrienne was upset about Irving's weight, what really made her mad was his attitude. "Irving doesn't care how I feel or what I think," she said. "If he were bothered by something about me, I'd change it, because I want to make him happy. But not Irving! He doesn't give a damn. I told him I won't sleep with him again until he loses weight. I *can't*. When I see him naked, his rolls of fat gross me out." You'd think Adrienne's remarks would upset Irving. But instead of fuming, he let out a hearty laugh. "I'm happy with the way I look," he said, smiling. "I'm not going out for the Olympics. First of all, I have no complaints with Adrienne, so I wouldn't ask her to change anything about herself. I love her unconditionally. I'm disappointed that she can't love me the way I am." Adrienne tried another angle. "What about your health? Why aren't you worried about that?" she asked. "Your doctor told you that your blood pressure and blood sugar are high. Do you think I want to be a widow?" Irving laughed once again. "Don't worry," he said, patting her arm. "If I die, you'll be rich."

Thanks to Adrienne, the couple stayed in treatment long enough to discover that they shared a *giving vs. withholding* conflict, but they couldn't make substantial progress in grappling with it. Even so, they decided to stay together. Adrienne remained angry with Irving and pledged never to have sex with him again, and Irving kept on eating and decided that he could live without sex.

You may not think that this is a healthy resolution, and certainly their lives would have been substantially improved if they had been able to wrestle with their conflict and get better control of it. But every couple has to make the best choice it can, and such resolutions can work for some people. I should caution, however, that this may be only a temporary fix that serves a couple's purposes due largely to considerations other than what they really desire for the relationship. In the case of Harold and Esther, they were senior citizens and Harold had significant health problems. There was less chance they'd end up splitting after all because at such a late age they had so much to lose if they did.

Parents of young children also are more likely to reach an agreement—or to compromise on their option choice—because they are reluctant to put their kids through the trauma of a divorce. But in my clinical experience, many of these couples only put their differences on hold and then split up once their kids are more independent. These couples *may* or *may not* be conscious that they plan to terminate their relationship. Some mates plot out the exact time and place that they'll tell their partner the marriage is over, but others surprise even themselves when they finally decide to leave. When I've asked clients what led them to call it quits, I often get a vague answer. "I don't really know," one woman told me. "I woke up one morning and said to myself, 'I've had enough.' I was just as surprised as my husband when I announced my decision." It may feel like a surprise, but people like this former client usually don't realize the future consequences of a failure to gain as much control over their conflict as possible. The more unruly a master conflict is, the greater the chances are that it will find an opportunity to strike, such as when the kids are grown and out of the house.

I once saw a couple who totally disagreed on their choice of options. The husband wanted to work on fixing the relationship at its core, while the wife didn't want to change a thing. Because the couple had seven children, they decided to leave their differences be for the foreseeable future and focus on raising their family together. After putting most of their kids through private high school and college, they came to see me to break up; they still hadn't been able to work through.

Also be aware that it may turn out that one or the other of you says you are committed to working on your master conflicts but isn't truly up for the hard work. You may think you've made a decision when you haven't. This is more common than you realize—my clients do it all the time. A decision is made on two levels: *emotional* and *intellectual*. So, you may *tell* yourself (or somebody else) that you've made up your mind, but your heart may not be in sync with your decision. Listen to Phil's story. After several couples sessions with me, Phil, fifty, a fast-talking, charismatic salesman, said that he'd decided to forgive his second wife, Roxanne, a forty-two-year-old office manager of a dental practice, for having had an affair with her boss. To her credit, Roxanne did all the right things to save the couple's ten-year marriage: confess to her affair rather than get caught red-handed; stop the affair immediately after confessing to it; swear her allegiance to Phil and her marriage; and commit to go to therapy with Phil to work on the relationship so that she wouldn't cheat again. Perfect. For his part, Phil agreed to work on the marriage, accept his contribution to the long-standing marital problems that had played some role in the development of the affair, and stop obsessing about Roxanne's infidelity. Fine. Phil attended every session with Roxanne, and I was optimistic that this marriage could be saved.

Week after week I would listen to this couple try to figure

out their mutual master conflict. Still, something was very wrong. Phil never mentioned the affair, yet he picked on little things in the relationship that seemed, at least to me, trivial. For example, Roxanne, meaning well, surprised Phil with tickets to a romantic opera. Instead of being happy with Roxanne's effort, he called her behavior "manipulative"—just another way to get control of his feelings. As I told Phil, "Even if Roxanne's behavior was a little manipulative, it was manipulative in a good way. She's trying desperately to get the marriage back on track." Nothing I said was getting through—Phil was in another place.

What made their therapy challenging was Phil's inconsistency. Some weeks he'd seem fine—and claim to be so. Other times he was back to his old tricks. His favorite technique was to misinterpret what Roxanne said and then use his misinterpretation as an excuse to get mad at her. For example, Roxanne told Phil that his sixteen-year-old son from his first marriage couldn't visit on a particular day because she had haircuts scheduled for *their* six-year-old twins. Phil went ballistic, claiming that Roxanne was always trying to alienate Phil's son, who lived several miles away. He said that Roxanne never wanted him around and was trying to get him out of Phil's life. Roxanne was shocked. She loved her stepson and explained that the haircut appointments had been scheduled well in advance of his son's request to visit. If Phil would be home, Roxanne said, his son would be welcome to come over, but she and the kids wouldn't be there. Phil called this "bullshit," insisting that Roxanne was trying to stay out of the house so she wouldn't have to see his son. Bottom line: Phil thought he made a decision to save his marriage, but it seemed that he was desperately trying to fight with Roxanne. When I confronted Phil as to whether he was comfortable about his decision to rescue his marriage, he confessed: "I tried to forget about the affair but I can't . . . I just can't let it go and I doubt I ever will. As much as I'd like to make this marriage work, I think it's over. I guess you could say it was over the day she started her affair." So, Phil thought he made up his mind to change and to save his marriage, but in reality he didn't. This was made evident by his sabotaging behavior.

IF YOU DECIDE TO BREAK APART

The simple truth is that not all relationships can be made to work, nor should they all. Not every couple can work through their conflicts. They may try and try, but they just might not be able to get them under control enough to save their relationship. That's reality; not all relationships can be rescued. For some, the symptoms may be too severe to overcome, such as physical abuse; in others, they may be too ingrained to work through. But that's no excuse for considering yourself a failure. I hear this self-deprecating attitude far too often in my practice. Those who recently divorced or are about to divorce—especially if they didn't initiate or want the split—are really good at beating themselves up. Many feel they should have been able to save their relationships, even if their partners weren't as committed to the rescue process. Try very hard not to do this to yourself. So you're not perfect. At least you had the courage to take on one of the toughest challenges on the planet. And the end of the relationship may well be the best result.

Consider Ty and Jasmine, who came for therapy because Jasmine, a feisty forty-four-year-old teacher, felt that Ty, a thirty-eight-year-old insurance agent, wasn't "pulling his weight" in the marriage. "My job is just as demanding as Ty's, but he never takes care of the kids, cooks, or cleans the house," she complained. "As a matter of fact, he hangs with his buddies at a bar in the city every day after work, and sometimes he doesn't even show his face until nine p.m. I'm tired of this. He needs to make up his mind whether he wants to be a married man or an adolescent and be with his posse." Ty rolled his eyes. "I just can't take her anymore," he said. "She acts like my mother. I don't need another mother. My mother and sisters raised me. I've had enough women telling me what to do in my life." Jasmine shook her head in disgust. "Well, if you act like a teenager," she said, "you're going to be treated like one."

Though Jasmine was hopping mad, she was committed to improving her marriage. Ty, on the other hand, was skeptical. The couple stayed in treatment long enough to come to a mutual understanding that their problems were being caused largely by a *getting one's needs met vs. caretaking* shared conflict, but Ty announced one night that he really didn't feel like "doing anything different." His view was "I am who I am. She can take me like this or forget it." Jasmine didn't want a separation, but she realized that she'd end up overworking the rest of her life if she stayed with Ty. So she reluctantly decided that a divorce would be in both their best interests.

An important point here is that you must not let your partner stop you from making a healthy decision. If your partner is not willing to do the work to improve your relationship, in most cases, you should not just accept that you have to live with your problems. Ending your relationship can be a perfectly valid choice. Not everybody is built for insight; not everybody can fix things. Don't fantasize that your partner is more than he or she really is. I always tell my clients who want to get into a new relationship that everybody has problems. There is no such thing as a "perfect person." But if you're a person who has grown interested in insight and self-knowledge, and your partner doesn't want to look at him- or herself in such depth, then moving on may well be advised. I know some therapists who believe that change in one partner will bring about change in the other. I say maybe, and maybe not. You'll need to judge for yourself, and keep in mind that you may lose years of potential happiness by staying in a bad relationship that has no real prospect of being fixed. The work of diagnosing your own inner conflicts will not have been wasted, however. With your newfound knowledge about your master conflict, you understand relationships better than you did before, and you've developed skills to help you better achieve your relationship goals. In my practice I've seen people rebound from breakups and end up a good deal better off than before. Here are stories of two couples I've treated who endured painful splits. In both cases the partner who continued to work on their own master conflict found happiness in a new relationship.

Maggie, thirty-six, came to see me by herself because her husband of fifteen years, Dylan, thirty-eight, "didn't believe in therapy." Maggie complained that Dylan was emotionally abusive. "He has a terrible temper," she said. "Anything can set him off. He calls me names and ridicules me in front of our children and I can't take it anymore. I don't get it, I do *everything* for him, and I get abuse in return. What about my needs?" Through Maggie, I learned that Dylan felt she overreacted. "He thinks I'm too sensitive," she said. "He just doesn't see the pain he causes." Although I recommended marital therapy for the couple, Dylan held his ground and refused treatment. Maggie used therapy to uncover and get control of her *getting your needs met vs. caretaking* conflict, and after six months she filed for divorce.

Maggie went through the usual gyrations during the divorce

process, including anxiety about money problems and the divorce's impact on the couple's two children, eleven and nine. But what she worried about most was her ability to find a man someday who'd treat her with love and respect. She was afraid of marrying another man like her ex-husband—a common concern of the newly divorced.

After another four months of therapy, Maggie began to date. Initially she chose men like her ex-husband—men who were unable to meet her needs. But as she gained more insight and control of her master conflict (how it was related to her verbally abusive mother and selfish father), a life-changing shift occurred. She began to date well-educated, well-spoken, kind men who were happy to take care of her. After her first date with one such man, she felt weird. "I'm just not used to this kind of guy," she told me, shaking her head. Despite her discomfort, Maggie hung in there, and within two years, she fell in love with a wonderful man and got remarried. And yes, from the way Maggie described him, he probably had a caretaker conflict as well; his first wife was apparently abusive. But instead of being an abusive "taker," he was a reformed caretaker who had been in therapy for several years. Maggie calls once in a while to give me an update on her life and the reports are all good.

The second story is a little more complicated. Scott, forty-two, and Andrea, thirty-eight, were fighting over money. Scott, a landscape architect with his own business, said that Andrea overspent and that she was going to send him to the poorhouse. "She maxed out all of our credit cards, and she buys a lot of crap that we don't even need," he fumed. "I have over forty thousand dollars in credit card balances alone and the interest keeps piling up. I don't know what to do with her." Andrea was unapologetic: "Most of the stuff that I buy, we need. Scott just worries too much. I think he needs medication to calm down."

Andrea wasn't thrilled with being in therapy. Ironically, she said that it was a bill the couple really didn't need. But she continued treatment for several months, hoping to get Scott to "get off her back about money." This never happened, of course. So she eventually left Scott and filed for divorce.

At the time of the split, Scott was making strides to conquer his *success vs. sabotage* master conflict, which he had developed courtesy of a successful father who always put him down. But unfortunately, he stopped treatment when Andrea left him. While I warned him of the potential for replicating his mate choice, he disappeared. Not a peep out of Scott for about two years, and then one day my phone rang. The reason for the distress call: Scott was struggling on the dating scene. "I'm scared," he said. "I thought I was going to be fine, but I'm really too afraid I'll pick someone like Andrea."

Scott dated infrequently in the years immediately following his divorce—his anxiety had really gotten the best of him. But Bonnie, twenty-eight, the one woman with whom he became serious during this time, turned out to be a shopaholic. Unlike Scott's ex-wife, Bonnie, a sales executive, earned a good salary, but she spent it all between paychecks.

Although the experience undermined Scott's already shaky confidence, his decision to end his relationship with Bonnie turned out to be a good move: it motivated him to reenter therapy and do more much-needed work on his *success vs. failure* master conflict.

Scott stayed on in therapy. But after about a year, guess what happened? He disappeared again. Five years passed before he next got in touch with me. "I think I did pretty well this time, but I could use a couples session with my new wife," he said. Oh no!

What now, I thought? A woman who invests in penny stocks? To my surprise, Scott was right. He did do "well." He had consciously decided to remarry a woman with a good business mind. Rachel knew how to run a business, having worked in her family's successful catering business for many years. And she was frugal. There was no way Rachel was going to reduce Scott's financial stature. In fact, Scott had expanded his business since I had seen him last and was admittedly doing quite well financially. "We have our kids' college paid for already," Scott boasted. Made sense to me! With Rachel in charge of his books, Scott couldn't fail. So why did Scott want a session?

If you follow my theory, for Rachel to have been attracted enough to Scott to marry him, she too must have had at least some form of a *success vs. sabotage* master conflict. And she did. Rachel's conflict showed itself in being *too* frugal, although she made lots of money. In other words, she could achieve success by making a lot of money but still feel like a failure and act as if she didn't have enough to enjoy herself. Because Scott had a reasonable amount of control over his conflict, he was able to marry someone who could help him become a success, but he wanted to celebrate his accomplishments. Scott felt that although Rachel was a real step-up from his ex and Bonnie, he wasn't having any fun in life. Turns out that Rachel's conflict needed a little tweaking so that she and Scott could enjoy the fruits of their labor. This took about three months of treatment, and the couple went on their merry way.

If you've recently ended a long-term relationship or marriage, or are in the process of doing so, I'll bet you'd like your life story to end as well as Maggie's and Scott's. The next section will give you more specific pointers on what to look for in a new partner before you take the plunge again.

CHOOSING A NEW PARTNER: DOING IT BETTER THE NEXT TIME

Some people are traumatized after a significant relationship falls apart. They put their lives on hold for fear of repeating the same mistakes and ending up with the same results. Some of these people wait years to reenter the dating world; others never date again—they isolate themselves or put their energy into friends, family, or career. I don't necessarily blame them. Losing a long-term relationship or marriage is usually a traumatic experience. I'm frequently asked by clients, How can I avoid another separation or divorce? How will I be able to find someone I can spend the rest of my life with? I'm no guru. And I certainly can't predict the future with 100 percent accuracy. But I do have some suggestions, and the first one is predictable: **Know your master conflict.**

Sounds familiar, right? If you understand your master conflict and know how it impacts your relationships, you'll have a much greater chance of choosing a more suitable partner. Most of the clients I've treated attempt to analyze the person they're dating. I've even had a few divorced clients—both male and female—ask me to check out their dates to make sure they were suitable. (I try to avoid this situation; it has a sneaky quality.) I prefer that my clients work on themselves instead—it's much more foolproof. Now, I'm not suggesting that you shouldn't take a good look at the person you're considering for a long-term relationship. In fact, we'll soon go over a few key questions you should answer before you engage in a serious relationship. But you *must* realize that this type of analysis (even with my help) will not offer you the highest level of protection against replicating the mistakes you made in your previous relationship. First of all, because you're probably not a professional at this sort of thing, your analysis will be limited. Second, I won't be there to help you analyze the information you've gathered. Third, the process is exhausting, especially if you're dating more than one person. And fourth, how in the world will you find out all you need to know about the person anyway? How much time do you have to investigate?

Don't sweat it. If your master conflict is under control, you'll automatically choose someone whose conflict is at about the same level of intensity as your own. That's the way it works. With two relatively well-controlled master conflicts, you and your partner should get yourselves out of most relationship jams—and that's what you should aim to achieve. If your master conflict is out of control (or having a consistently negative impact on your relationships), your radar will be off, and you'll invariably choose someone with the same rowdy master conflict. Simply put: Know your conflict, get it under control, and let your radar do the work.

Now, as promised, let's take a look at some of the key questions that I believe will help you to measure the potential suitability of a healthy long-term partner. While this section is geared toward those who may be on their second (or more) long-term relationship or marriage, many of these suggestions will apply if you're single and looking for your first life mate:

- *Are you physically attracted to your partner?* *While your master conflict will draw you to your partner, it may not be for reasons of physical attraction. I believe it's important that you be honest with yourself in determining whether you are "really" attracted to, and have a passion for, this person. Sexual compatibility is vital for most couples. I've seen too many partners underestimate the importance of a good sex life, only to regret it later. Lack of sexual compatibility is also a prime reason for extramarital affairs.*

- **Can your partner take responsibility for their actions or behaviors?** *Nobody's perfect. But if your mate can't or won't acknowledge their shortcomings, you could be headed for a life fraught with control struggles. It's important that your partner be able to admit when they are wrong and be able to apologize.*

- **Can your partner express feelings, and if so, how?** *Certainly you'll want your partner to be able to express love and devotion, but one of your biggest concerns should be how they express anger. Living with someone who has little self-control and impulsively explodes, or a passive-aggressive mate who carries out sneak attacks, can both be nightmares.*

- **Does the level of closeness your partner seems most comfortable with fit with your own?** *Some people simply can't tolerate much distance in a relationship—they feel abandoned. Others can't tolerate much closeness—they feel as if there is a noose around their neck. It would be wise to assess your own intimacy needs and compare and contrast them to those of your partners. You'll want to match up well here or you could be in for chronic pursuer-distancer cycle—one of you will be constantly pursuing the other for closeness, while the other always looks for an escape hatch.*

- **Has your potential partner ever been married or in a long-term relationship before, and if so, for how long?**

Taking the plunge helps to ensure that the partner you've chosen was healthy enough to risk commitment. People over forty who have never been in a long-term relationship or marriage are a higher risk. The longer your partner was married, the less risky they would be to invest in. I think ten years or longer is a good indication that a person is somewhat capable of a commitment, provided of course there wasn't a lengthy separation during that period. Some couples are married for four years and don't divorce for another four.

- **Who divorced whom?** *If your partner has a history of dumping people, beware! You could be next. Some dumpers have a lot of unresolved anger and use the dumping method as a way to retaliate. Others dump before there's any chance of being rejected—this is often a result of insecurity.*

- **Has your partner come from a divorced home?** *Children of divorce are more likely to divorce in their adulthood. Fighting hard to save a marriage may not have been role-modeled for them. Having already experienced it, they may be less afraid of it as well. I'm not suggesting that you shy away from someone whose parents divorced—this would reduce your pool of potential partners beyond reason. But you might try to determine the impact this experience has had on your partner and how it has shaped their view of a long-term commitment or marriage in particular. If your partner is able to view their parents' divorce from a rational and objective point of view (e.g., seeing each parent's contribution to the demise of the marriage), the less chance there is that the divorce trauma will have a negative effect on your current relationship.*

- *Is your partner close to their parent of the opposite sex?*
  While your choice of mate can be equally affected by your rela-
  tionship with either of your parents, I believe the relationship
  your partner has with the opposite-sex parent gives you a bet-
  ter indication of how you'll be treated. For example, most of the
  men I've counseled who had healthy relationships with their
  mothers seemed to have more respect for women and tended to
  treat their wives and girlfriends better than those who didn't.

- *Does your partner have any addictions?* *This can lead to a*
  life of hell, so even if you have no idea what your master con-
  flict is, avoid this problem if you can. This doesn't mean that you
  should reject people in recovery. But take into account their com-
  mitment to treatment and where they are in their treatment pro-
  cess. I'd recommend that you refrain from making a commitment
  to anyone until you're sure of their sobriety for at least a year.

- *Does your partner share your life interests?* *I thought that*
  as long as two people loved one another, they didn't need to have
  a lot in common. I figured it would be nice to have shared inter-
  ests, but not vital. Silly me! I'm now convinced that the more
  you have in common with your partner, the better your rela-
  tionship will be. I'm not referring just to hobbies; I also mean
  a shared energy level and a shared passion for life. A client
  recently told me that he was ending his engagement to a woman
  because although they golfed and skied together, her energy level
  was a lot lower than his.

- *Does your partner share your life goals?* *Does your partner*
  want to remarry someday or do they prefer to be cohabitating

lovers? Does he or she want more children? Where do you want to live? I treated one couple—a second marriage for each— who couldn't agree on whether to live in Pennsylvania (near her relatives) or move to Illinois (for its better job opportunities). Where do you want to be in ten or twenty years? Do you want to retire and live on a beach or would you like to own an apartment in New York City? Do you want to play golf every day or would you prefer to continue working until the company security guard carries you out of the office? I believe it's important to have a shared vision of the future. I treated a couple in their early seventies who decided to separate because he wanted to move to Florida and build his dream house, while she wanted to stay in New Jersey and remain close to her children and grandchildren.

- **Does your partner want to add more children to their life?** *In my experience, people don't discuss this topic in enough depth. If you have children, make sure your potential partner has the tolerance to cope with the issues that will present themselves in a remarried or reconstituted family. If the shoe is on the other foot, be honest with yourself in determining whether you want to take more on. Children can be a major factor in a couple's success or failure, especially if they have significant problems or if your partner's ex is difficult.*

- **Do you think your partner is in love with you?** *Although lots of people can say they love their partner, not nearly as many can say that they're "in love" with them. It's a tricky subject, but you can begin to tackle it by asking yourself whether you feel that your potential partner seems to really enjoy being around* *you and treats you as if you are special. Do you get a sense that there's no other place (s)he'd rather be than with you and that there's no other person (s)he'd rather be with? When you make love, does it seem as if (s)he is truly present and concerned about pleasing you? You might also want to ask yourself whether the closeness or distance you desire seems to match up with the closeness or distance (s)he feels comfortable with.*

LAST THOUGHTS

I hope that this book has enabled you to reach a new understanding of the problems in your relationship and that it has provided you with a way forward in trying to repair it. Or perhaps it has helped you determine that the right course for you is to get out of your relationship and look for a happier and healthier one. As I said at the very beginning of the book, all relationships are complex, and it can be daunting to diagnose the sources of troubles and then do the daily work to bring about change. Certainly, the discovery that you and your partner share a master conflict is no magic bullet. You may or may not be able to find a way to manage your conflict better. But I encourage you to make a serious commitment to the process and to fight back whatever discouragement you may feel along the way. Change will surely take time, but I have seen it come for many couples I've counseled, and you should take heart because by reading this book and searching for a solution, you have taken an important first step.

ACKNOWLEDGMENTS

I knew I couldn't lose with two great literary agents in my corner. Elisabeth Weed, thank you so much for recommending me as a client to Holly Root. If it weren't for both of you, this book would probably never have seen the light of day. Holly has been a super agent: assertive, empathic, knowledgeable, patient, present, and positive. I couldn't have asked for a better experience than I received and continue to receive from Holly and her colleagues at the Waxman Literary Agency. I feel blessed to be with the best.

Speaking of the best, my editor at Simon & Schuster, Emily Loose, amazed me with her speed in grasping the clinical concepts in this book. And her ability in helping me clarify my theories and interventions made them easier even for me to understand. I will never forget Emily's dedication to this project. Thanks for believing in me, Emily. It's been an honor to work with you and your terrific staff, especially production editor Edith Lewis and Anne Cherry, my most skilled and insightful copyeditor.

I've been working with writer extraordinaire Cynthia Hanson on *Ladies' Home Journal*'s "Can This Marriage Be Saved?" column for more than eight years and we're still at it. A friend as well as a colleague, Cynthia was also instrumental in the initial development of my proposal. She took time out of her hectic schedule to copyedit the entire manuscript before I had the nerve to submit it to be reviewed for publication. I will always relish Cynthia's seal of approval. While her name isn't on the cover, it is in spirit.

And finally, my daughters Jennifer and Melanie have always been an inspiration to me, but I must give special mention to Melanie, who, lo and behold, wants to become a psychiatrist. I wish you only the best as you pursue your dream. I truly believe that you've got the key ingredients for the work: the ability to empathize, and of course, talent.

INDEX

ABOUT THE AUTHOR

Stephen J. Betchen completed his doctorate at the University of Pennsylvania School of Social Work (now the School of Social Policy & Practice) with a specialization in marriage and family therapy. He subsequently completed fellowships in sex therapy and psychoanalysis. He is a licensed marriage and family therapist and a certified sex therapist with a practice in Cherry Hill, New Jersey, specializing in couples therapy. Dr. Betchen is the author of numerous professional articles on relationships and the well-received book *Intrusive Partners-Elusive Mates: The Pursuer-Distancer Dynamic in Couples.* In addition, he is a contributor to the popular *Ladies' Home Journal* column "Can This Marriage Be Saved?"

Printed in the United States
By Bookmasters